ACKNOWLEDGMENTS

For more than fifty years I have been interested in coyotes, ever since the first time I heard one howl on the North Dakota prairie where I grew up. During that span of more than half a century, many people have taught me many things about coyotes. Where do I start to list them and acknowledge their help? Obviously, that would be a total impossibility—to list all who have fed information into me, and thus changed my total opinion about coyotes. I am indebted to so many, and wish to thank a few publicly—for helping me to learn.

Many professionals answered my questions and sent me copies of long-forgotten data and old reports, and this has lent accuracy and authenticity to my work. Professionals like Norton Miner, Dr. Franz Camenzind, Bill Fitzwater, Rew Van Hanson, Bill Pfeiffer, Dr. Bart W. O'Gara, Guy Connolly, Jim Keefe, Sam Linhart, Weldon Robinson, Don Balser, and Tom Mussehl—and many more. I apologize for not listing so many others.

I would also like to acknowledge the information gained from working with a different group of professionals—the men who worked on the trap line against coyotes, who flew the planes and placed the 1080 stations—hundreds of them. Especially high on that list would be South Dakota personnel from District Agent Mark D. Worcester on down through Pilot Walden Lemm, to field personnel like Bob Burgee, Ralph Block, Dean Badger, Cecil Albers, Bill Pullins, George Barnes; and a very great host of Texas *coyoteros*—especially subdistrict supervisor Calvin Johnson, and the other subdistrict bosses—E. G. Pope, Johnny White, Hinton Bridgwater, Darwin (Shorty) Ivy, Jimmy Ellard, and Jimmy Poore, along with their right hand aides—Carl Baker, Tom Sparks, Byrl Bierschwale, and Roy McBride. Government trappers in Texas all taught me something about coyotes (and the killing of them) but I'd especially like to thank Frank Martin, who still holds the record for killing more coyotes in a year than any other man; Big Earl Baker, Wayne McRorey, George Schacherl, Agapito Flores and Gumercindo Rezendez and Louis Gerland and at least a hundred others.

And I'd like to thank the men who taught me as I worked under their supervision, especially Regional Director John C. Gatlin, Regional Supervisor E. C. Cates and District Agent Mark D. Worcester. These men not only gave me the opportunity to learn, but they also encouraged me in new approaches, in studying new methods—and even approving of my attempts to write about the battle against coyotes and about the interesting animal itself. In thanking this small part of the army of men who have contributed to my store of knowledge of coyotes, I do not wish that any blame for my opinions be assigned to them. I have come to my own conclusions and formed my own opinions.

I would also like to thank the millions of coyotes who have contributed their expertise—thank them for the thousands of times that they have outwitted me. They have made me wiser and humbler. Mr. Coyote, I salute you. You are a survivor; you always will be!

TABLE OF CONTENTS

INTRODUCTION

A number of years ago I had the pleasure of hunting on a Wyoming sheep ranch. My host was a gracious, elderly gentleman who started as a sheep herder and parlayed his meager beginnings into a Texas-styled ranch. It was a pleasure to be in his company and to discuss subjects of the day—until I mentioned coyotes. The subject of coyotes completely changed his personality; in short, the only good coyote was a dead one!

As an urbanite and an easterner, I was shocked at the man's vindictiveness against coyotes. But with the passage of time, the reason for his emotional tirades came into sharp focus for me. He had seen too many of his sheep and lambs killed by the "gray ghost" of the plains.

Many books have been written on the controversial coyote, but none have approached the sensitivity of writing, nor have the authors had the personal experience of Chuck Cadieux, and for good reason. Besides being a gifted writer and outdoorsman, Chuck Cadieux has spent almost his entire life in coyote country and was involved in coyote control for the U.S. Fish and Wildlife Service for more than a decade. He not only kept careful notes of his field experience, but learned from his co-workers. Interlaced with endless anecdotes and personal experience, the text of the book flows.

Chuck Cadieux does not judge man's many, and sometimes highly controversial, control methods. Rather, he presents them without emotion and lets the reader determine the necessity and humaneness of the control technique.

This fine book will provide the reader with a better understanding and appreciation of the coyote—and man's eternal battle to control their numbers.

Edward L. Kozicky
October 14, 1982

Chapter 1

What We Know about Coyotes

The Random House dictionary of the English language defines a coyote as: *"A carnivorous, wolflike animal, also called prairie wolf,* Canis latrans *of western North America, noted for its loud and prolonged howling at night. (2) in American Indian legend, the culture hero and trickster of the American Indians of the West. (3) Slang, a contemptible person, a cheat."*

My dictionary also goes further to ascribe the origin of the name "coyote" to the Nahuatl Indians word, "coyotl." In the same dictionary, there is a drawing of a coyote along with a caption informing us that the animal is about three and a half feet long, with one foot of that length being its tail, and that it stands about a foot and a half high at the shoulder.

That is a mighty sparse and incomplete definition of this animal. In the following pages of this book, we will try to round out the description of the most adaptable and successful life form in the realm of North American mammals. Let's start with some basics. That foot long tail is usually much longer than twelve inches in the adult; it is bottle-shaped and almost always carried low—in the "skulking" position. The word "skulking" seems to have been coined for the purpose of describing the motions of the coyote—an animal which has learned that its safety lies in not being noticed by man.

Hope Ryden (author, student of wildlife, and writer for the

1

National Geographic) and other glamorizers of the coyote like to call him by his Indian name—"God's Dog." The coyote's kinship to the domestic canine is apparent to the most casual observer.

How big is a coyote? Size variations are great in the groups of subspecies that make up the coyote clan. I've weighed fully grown adults in northern Coahuila in old Mexico that averaged twelve pounds, despite a bountiful supply of rabbits and other rodents. In Archer County, Texas, we found very large coyotes in 1960–1961. A dozen specimens averaged 43 pounds! Milton Caroline, who spent the major part of his working life in charge of predator control in Texas, feels that this Archer County group was the remnant of a particular hybridization with one of the larger members of the wolf family.

What color is a coyote? Jim Keefe (Chief of Information for the Missouri Department of Conservation) calls the coyote, "The Outcast in Gray" in his excellent article about the coyote in Missouri, reprinted elsewhere in this book. Colors vary greatly, although 99 percent of all coyotes are a reddish or brownish gray, shading almost to black, shading almost to red, and shading completely to white at times. Although albinism in coyotes is

extremely rare, there were three pure white coyotes taken in western North Dakota during the fifteen year period ending in 1960. Government trapper Marvin Ingman took the last one on a coyote-getter in 1959.

Where are the coyotes? When Christopher Columbus started the despoliation of this continent by announcing to Europeans that it really existed, the range of the coyote was limited to the semi-arid, almost treeless plains which stretched westward from Minnesota to the Rockies and from central Kansas and central Texas across the great southwestern desert to southern California. His range also stretched across the high, dry central plateau of northern Mexico and down into the Baja California peninsula.

A closely related species, *Canis niger,* occupied a similar ecological niche east of the coyotes' range, stretching from eastern Texas to Florida and the Carolinas, with goodly populations in all of the intervening states. Larger than the coyote with bigger bone structure, a larger head (proportionally), and a completely different look about it, the red wolf could interbreed with the coyote. During the past few centuries when the red wolf numbers were dwindling before the remorseless assault of mankind, the coyote prospered, increased, and expanded his range. As the red wolf found it harder to locate a mate, interbreeding with coyotes has become more common. In 1982 there is little likelihood that there is a single red wolf individual that does not carry coyote genes in its makeup. There no longer is a "pure" red wolf. Perhaps there never was!

I know of no reliable account of coyotes interbreeding with the much larger timber wolf. They do interbreed with many types and breeds of domestic dogs. I have observed several litters of "coyogs" or "doyotes" and noticed that the hybrid does not possess the endurance and vigor of their coyote parent. You often find nervous, excitable young canines, ill-suited to being pets—and equally unsuited to earning a living as the coyote does.

Most domestic dogs will attack the so-called "God's dog" upon sight, though most domestic dogs find the fierce little coyote more than a match in a one-on-one fight. Some of the sight-running hounds are trained to dispatch the coyote and are experts at it. They should be, for they outweigh the little coyote by three or four to one.

The early distribution of coyotes was limited to the intermountain west, east of the Rockies and west of the forested areas in the north (western Minnesota); west of the forested areas (a line running from western Iowa through western Missouri, Western Arkansas and into Texas), and across to the Pacific Coast in the southern part of its range. But coyotes ranged to the north, well into Saskatchewan, Alberta and Manitoba—they were found there when the first European explorers came through what is now Canada. Coyotes were also well known in Mexico, even from before the days of Cortez and the conquistadores. They are now found all the way south to Costa Rica. Tourists taking home coyote pups as pets have introduced these adaptable coyotes to the eastern United States. These animals are now in every one of the continental United States.

According to popular mythology, coyotes mate for life. True, there are instances of this happening, but the pair bond seems much weaker in "pack" conditions than when coyotes are scarce. When a female coyote is in heat, she may be bred only by the dominant male; others may be bred by every male in the vicinity. There is seldom a serious battle between males for the favors of the female, but rather there is a system in which the female selects her sexual partner, simply by savagely fighting off unwelcome males. In Duval County, Texas, I watched one wild female copulate with three different males in the same afternoon—complete the breeding action to the point of the copulatory "tie" or hanging up, common to canines. The three males did not seem to be vying for the privilege of breeding, but rather seemed to be patiently waiting their turn.

Trained observers have often documented the fact that a strong pair bond exists between male and female coyotes, a bond which has been proven to last for several years, or even for life—in some studies. Mortality is high among the coyote family, and it is very doubtful that a widowed coyote would long remain celibate. In fact there is evidence that coyote pairs do shift during their lifetimes. There is a very complicated social structure (larger than nuclear families) developed within stable groups of coyotes.

During the 1970s Dr. Franz J. Camenzind studied the social structure of coyotes on the National Elk Refuge in Wyoming as part of his doctoral investigations. He worked in a very specialized—one might say "unnatural"—environment. The Elk Refuge coyote was afforded almost complete protection from man, and had access to an almost unlimited supply of winter food—the carrion resulting from natural mortality of 7,500 or more wintering elk.

Despite the "unnatural" setting for his studies, Camenzind did

Always alert, the coyote is seldom seen silhouetted, but tries to remain as inconspicuous as possible at all times.

a thorough job. His observations about social structures among coyotes are well worth studying. His doctoral thesis cited his findings as follows:

The coyotes of the National Elk Refuge (NER) were studied from February 1971 to June 1976. Peak winter concentrations of coyotes occurred in February and March ($X = 0.73$ coyotes/ km^2), and by the April-May whelping season coyote densities reached their lowest ($X = 0.4$ coyotes/km^2). The average litter size was 4.45 and the average postwhelping density was 1.37 coyotes per km^2.

The NER coyote population was made up of four segments: nomads, aggregations, resident pairs and resident packs. The resident pairs and packs (three to seven coyotes) occupied and defended clearly defined territories by fighting and chasing intruders (direct defense) and by scent marking and vocalizing (indirect defense). Pack cohesiveness as well as all territorial activities varied seasonally and reached their zenith during the winter months (January to March).

Superimposed upon the range of the territorial coyotes were nomadic individuals who traveled within extensive home ranges. They were usually young of the year, disabled individuals and occasionally healthy adults.

Aggregations were large (7–22 coyotes) ephemeral groups that displayed no social organization and were composed of winter migrants and nomadic coyotes mingling with resident pairs and packs. Aggregations were observed only from November to early April and only near elk. They moved over existing territorial boundaries as resident coyotes seemed unable to effectively defend their boundaries or carrion food sources from the large numbers of coyotes.

What do coyotes eat? According to their advocates, coyotes live on only mice and harmful rodents, and cull out only the sick, old, and diseased animals from wild or domesticated ungulate herds. On the other hand, western sheepmen claim that coyotes eat only fat young lambs and pregnant ewes. Perhaps you've seen the bumper sticker which says, "Eat Lamb—50,000 coyotes can't be wrong!"

Dozens of studies have been made of the food habits of the coyote, and some of these will be detailed in Chapter 5. For the moment, let it be stated that the following have been found in coyote stomachs: mice, rabbits, shrews, voles, small birds, large game birds, eggs, snakes (both poisonous and non-poisonous), bats, lizards, iguanas, watermelon, tomatoes, lambs and ewes, kids and adult goats, deer, antelope, calves, belt buckles and straps, carrion of all kinds, lard, fish, frogs, grass, berries of all kinds, potatoes both cooked and raw, squash, grasshoppers by the millions, crickets—and the scats of other coyotes and the scats of bears.

The coyote will grow fat on many different diets—fish and grasshoppers in the grasslands, lamb in Wyoming's big ranches, turkeys in central Texas, snowshoe rabbits in the high country of Colorado and Utah, watermelons and crickets along the Rio Grande, road-killed carrion in Sinaloa and Chihuahua, and fat young fryers in Kansas. But the adaptable coyote can also exist on a very slim diet of lizards in the Sonoran desert, a single road-killed prairie dog in Wyoming, the leavings from a backpacker's campfire in the Gila Wilderness of New Mexico. The coyote can exist in the extreme cold of the northern plains and in the heat and fearful aridity of Mexico's high deserts. He will drink gallons per day from mountain streams, or exist on the scant juice in the withered bodies of jackrabbits on the Jornada del Muerte. More than any other characteristic, the coyote is adaptable.

Coyotes prosper where no other carnivore could find a meal to postpone inevitable starvation. He can eat from man's table, or thrive where man is unknown. He can live on man's herds of stupid sheep, or dine on the wildest speedsters of the plains—the pronghorned antelope. He will make-do with a diet of grass-hoppers at times. At other times he will kill sheep and lambs for the sport of hearing them bleat in terror before kicking their last. The coyote hunts successfully alone or in pairs, linked by their ventriloquial howls. At times he will hunt in packs, showing remarkable cooperation between pack members which are capable of running to earth and pulling down a mule deer buck in the prime of his life. He will solicitously bring mice to his young—regurgitating them for his pups to feed upon. He will also eat a new-born calf alive.

Indian tribes deified the coyote. Livestock operators curse him as being the devil incarnate—the reason they default on their mortgage and the kids can't go to college.

Whether cursed or worshipped, coyotes are here to stay. They have successfully endured man's attacks for centuries. This is a story of predators and survivors; a story of men versus coyotes. This is to be "their" book—*"COYOTES."*

Chapter 2

The Song of the Coyote

It would be wrong to call it a howling. There really isn't an accurate word to describe the wild, exciting, unearthly, weird, and eerie call of the coyote. Bull elk "bugling," is also a misnomer. The bull elk and the coyote have a common bond with their vocalization. Both elk and coyote start out with a couple of low-pitched sounds—grunts in the elk, yaps in the case of the coyote—which then go up in a suprisingly high pitched, wavering tremolo. Both animals make the hair stand up on the back of my neck, an atavistic reminder from the days my ancestors cowered in a cave and listened to the songs of the hunting packs.

There are overtones of the maniacal laughter of a hyena in the pre-dawn serenade of the coyote. Sometimes it starts out with a few sharp barks, such as might be written, "yap-yap-yap;" then immediately follows a "yowoooooooooeeeeeoooooeeee" series of marvelously long, drawn-out notes sustained in the higher register. Sometimes the serenader will just take time out for a breath and go right on singing, howl after howl. Our ears tell us a dozen animals must be out there in the darkness, but there may be only two. Coyotes often simply serenade the graying of dawn, promising to sing again that same evening when darkness returns.

In addition to its eerie falsetto, their howling is definitely ventriloquial in nature. I mean that it is very hard to determine from what direction the sound is coming. Three or four of us have stood listening to the song of the coyote many times. Upon its cessation, all of us simultaneously pointed to the origin of the song. We all pointed in different directions! This is especially true with pre-dawn singing when we are waiting for enough light to try calling the coyote to the gun—enough light to see the rifle sights.

Only once was I privileged to watch the singing of a wild coyote at close range. In the early January morning chill in Uvalde County, Texas, we stood in a *sendero,* waiting for enough light to go about our work. As a slight breeze carried our scent to the south, I had chosen a station against a big prickly pear cactus to avoid silhouetting myself against the lightening sky. A coyote came trotting along the *sendero,* unaware that man had intruded upon his prickly pear and mesquite haven. At fifty yards, he stopped and pointed his muzzle skyward. There were a couple of sharp yaps at first, like a farm dog uncertain of his own authority. Then the jaws stretched wide and that weird ululating sound ascended into the heavens. He controlled the pitch by controlling the size of his mouth. As the coyote hit the high C above high C, his black nose pointed skyward with his lower jaw aiming almost straight down!

His serenade was answered by a like sound from the south. That response must have been what he was searching for, because he turned directly toward the source of the sound and melted into the shadows of the south Texas landscape.

The most memorable serenade I recall was provided by a group of strolling coyotes in the extreme southwestern corner of New Mexico. On a solo hunting trip for javelina, I had gotten up two hours before sunrise to prepare a big breakfast and to climb over a rocky ridge about five hundred feet high into the valley where I intended to hunt.

Finishing my second cup of coffee, I heard coyotes singing from the ridge behind me, but I paid it scant attention for my mind was focused on the coming hunt. As I started the careful climb up the rocky ridge in the darkness, I was surprised to hear the song coming from very close at hand, on both sides of me. I knew that I had nothing to fear from coyotes, but I found myself searching the dark shadows for signs of the skulkers who now seemed to surround me.

There was no mistaking the fact that they were following me as I worked my way up the ridge and down the other side. My guess was that they were simply curious about my intentions. With their educated noses, they learned a lot about me on my trip over the ridge. They serenaded each other back and forth until it was completely light. Then the song ended without my seeing a single member of the singing pack. A conservative estimate of the numbers of this merry band would have to be at least a dozen, because sound came from at least fifteen different places in rapid succession.

I must admit that I was more at ease after the singing stopped. Why? I really don't know.

Coyote signs were everywhere in the sandy washes I traveled in my search for javelina. There was also some lion sign here and there, distinctive enough to let me know that a cat and her cub were working the area. It was almost nine o'clock when I found a herd of 13 javelina, made the simple stalk, and shot a young boar. At the bark of my .22/250 rifle, a coyote sang from two hundred yards (who can really estimate?) behind me. They had evidently stayed with me after the sunrise stilled their serenade.

This area contained many coyotes as well as home for a pair of lions. The javelina herd was healthy, with more of the little tuskers around than I had seen elsewhere in New Mexico. There were a number of whitetails, the diminutive but regal Coues species. Cottontail rabbits were numerous and the bush was alive with Gambels quail. Why did so many game species prosper in this land with its very high coyote population and a pair of lions?

Could it be that predators do not control the numbers of prey species, but rather that the availability of prey controls the numbers of predators?

Chapter 3

A Coyote Believes his Nose

Icy cold and clear as a bell—one of those days which comes often to Nebraska in January. I had parked the car in the shelter of a highway cut and eased my way to the summit of a hill to hide by a pile of stones that had been painfully gleaned from the fields to the north. My clothing was all camouflage white, even strips of adhesive tape covered most of the barrel of my rifle. My intent was to call a coyote or two.

Before I reached the stone pile, I saw a movement far out on the shining white expanse of snow to the north. My 8×50 binoculars found the moving black spot on the glaring white—a big coyote slowly walking westward, across the arctic wind which blew in my face.

Crouching low, I hurried to the shelter of the stone pile and slid behind it. After catching my breath, I lifted one eye up to where I could see the coyote still walking slowly, investigating every bit of weed cover which stuck up through the snow. He was almost exactly one mile away, according to the section line fences which marked a thin black spidery web against the unbroken white of the snow. Certain that the coyote was too far upwind to hear the call, I left it in my chest pocket. Warmly dressed, I could afford to wait and see if some other chance presented itself.

Handicapped by the tears in my eyes from the wind, I tried to watch the coyote as he worked his way westward. A jackrabbit leaped from its hiding place, less than fifty feet in front of the coyote. This was not the lowly, tick-ridden, scrawny blacktailed jack of southern climes, but the lordly, big, powerful whitetailed jack of the northern tier. These jackrabbits average twice as heavy as the blacktail. The snow was packed hard enough for the jack to run upon without breaking through. His hind feet came up past his ears as he stretched out—his vest pocket really scooping up gravel—as he put distance between him and the coyote.

The coyote took off after him, also running smoothly atop the snow. He didn't stretch out in full-speed pursuit. Rather, it was a half-hearted, going-through-the-motions sort of run. The speeding pair went in a southeasterly direction, with the wind. Their course would bring them past me about three hundred yards to the east. After a two hundred yard wind sprint, the coyote slowed to a walk. The jack continued to bounce along, stretching his lead. Every ten or twelve hops he'd jump straight up in the air, looking back to see if the coyote was following. The rabbit went out of sight in a long shallow valley, where sagebrush speckled the white snow. The coyote walked with his head down a few more yards, then turned aside to dig a mouse out of the grass. He gulped the tiny morsel quickly, and unhurriedly headed south.

The range was now about two hundred and fifty yards and the big dog coyote seemed temptingly near when viewed through the scope. I decided against sending the little 55 grain bullet out against the strong wind. I eased the call to my lips and sent the agonized squall out into the wind, and the coyote's head snapped up. He pivoted around to face me, eyes searching for any sign of movement. I remained perfectly still. He stared towards me for a long two minutes—then turned back to his southbound trail. I hit the call again, and again he swung around to search for me. He stood for a long time, then turned to trot southward.

Twice more I sent the wailing invitation to an easy meal, but the coyote didn't even look around. He had heard something, but he really didn't trust his ears.

As he went out of sight in a little dip, I scurried around to the other side of the stone pile, so that it was now hiding me from sight. The coyote was now nearly a mile south of me, and a little bit to the east. That little bit east was important, for that was why he hadn't yet caught my scent borne by the wind which came from exactly north. The coyote came into sight again, now trotting on a southwesterly course that would bring him across my scent line in a few minutes. Knowing that my two chances were slim and none, I stood up. Almost a mile away, the coyote stopped and stared. I moved a bit. He stared some more. Then he continued on his way, only stopping to investigate each tuft of grass. He didn't believe his eyes at that distance.

I stood perfectly still and watched the coyote. He was nearly one mile south of me and approaching a "straight downwind of me" position. As he trotted along, mousing still held his attention. Suddenly he swung around and faced directly at me. His fur seemed to stand on end as his nose read the message from one mile north. Without hesitating, he began to run, ears flattened to his head, his body stretched out in panic as he headed for the east and some broken country to hide in.

He was still running hard with no sign of slowing, when he went out of sight three-quarters of a mile to the east. This coyote had scented me, on the wings of a very strong, ice-laden wind, at a distance of approximately one mile. He believed his nose, immediately and without question—not his eyes!

Chapter 4

Present Status of Coyotes

What is the present status of the coyote? How are they coping with mankind's attempts to exterminate them for three hundred years? They must be fighting off extinction in some remote corner of their range.

No way, friend. Coyotes now enjoy their largest territorial range. From Alaska to Quebec, from Panama to Baja California and almost all points between, coyotes have enlarged their range. Although scarce east of the Mississippi River, coyotes are probably found in every one of our continental United States. Coyotes have extended their range up into the cold north country. They reached Alaska about thirty years ago and are now found as far north as Nome! Looking southward, they range down into the hot humid country, as far as the steaming hot Yucatan, in the bone-dry deserts of western Mexico, the mountains of Nicaragua and El Salvador, and the grassy slopes of Central America all the way to Panama.

Biology teaches us that when a pressure is exerted downward on a species, that species reacts with an equal and upward pressure. After centuries of persecution, coyotes survive very easily and have become amazingly adaptable. When it appeared that the poison 1080 was reducing coyote numbers over much of the west, upward resistance became strong. When 1080 was banned in 1972, the upward resistance faced little pressure and the coyote numbers increased.

The arid wastelands of the desert southwest are home to the adaptable coyote.

Sheepmen have gone out of business in many parts of the western plains because the numerous coyotes eat more lambs than go to market. A fuller treatment of this situation will be found later in the book.

This upswing in coyote numbers fortunately came at a time when the price for their pelts was very high. In the early 1980s, coyote pelts sold for more than $100 each. Even before this inflation in coyote fur prices, the number of coyotes taken rose steadily. The state of Missouri has the Extension Trapper system, which was designed to quiet farmer and rancher complaints about coyote depredations, not reduce coyote numbers.

In 1958, Missouri reported that only seven coyote pelts were sold in the state. This is understandable; they were worth only twenty-five cents each. Double the price to fifty cents and we have a total coyote pelt sale in Missouri of nineteen animals in 1961. In 1965, the coyote price went all the way up to two bucks each, and the catch was 379 coyotes.

In 1972 the price was $9.55 on the average, and the total coyote take in Missouri was 9,217. Does this mean that the fur take is a direct factor of the price of the individual pelt? Or does it mean that in 1972 coyotes started being more numerous, thus easier to take? In 1973, the price went up to $10.40 and the catch went to 12,960. Price dropped to $7.20 in 1975, but the catch stayed up at 14,243—a bigger catch than in 1973, despite a 30 percent drop in the price per pelt. It begins to look like the numbers of available coyotes has more to do with the catch than the average price per pelt. In 1978, an average price of $27.70 brought a total catch of 20,705. Dropping the price to $18.80 in 1979 did not reduce the catch much—20,202 coyotes.

Starting in 1980, inflation raised all prices, and fashions dictated more demand for coyote pelts. In the winter of 1980–1981, coyote pelts sold for as much as $125. That price was often topped in the next two winters—and great numbers of coyotes were taken by fur trappers . . . both because the price was high and because there were plenty of coyotes.

How successful has the coyote species been? It surrounded the last islands of purebred red wolves and simply engulfed the entire gene pool. Through hybridization, the red wolf disappeared. The more successful coyote species may grin and say, "Thanks to the red wolf we'll probably be a little larger—but the centuries will breed that weakness out of us."

The numbers of coyotes killed by federal trappers never were a reliable indicator of the coyote population for several reasons. First, compound 1080 killed more coyotes than any other control method, yet its victims were seldom found and tallied. Lower kill figures in the years from 1945 through 1971 did not indicate decreased efficiency of the trapper force, but rather reflected unretrieved victims of 1080 and reduced numbers of coyotes upon which to count coup . . . again a function of compound 1080.

After the executive order in 1972 banned the use of 1080, kill figures stayed about the same, or rose slightly. The control program, forced to abandon its most effective tool, used more control methods (steel traps and coyote-getters) that allowed retrieval and tabulation of nearly every coyote killed.

The total kill figures of the federal program (discussed at great length later in the book) only suggest that one cannot kill and scalp coyotes if they are not present to be killed and scalped. "Are there coyotes available for the taking today?" does not seem to be the appropriate question to put to the federal programmers.

In the nine years after 1080 was banned in 1981, the federal certified catch has fluctuated from a low of 71,300 in 1972 to a high of 84,499 in 1976 and back to a real low of 57,178 in 1981. The low figure of 1981 reflects reduced effort on the part of the federal program—not by their choice, but because of budgetary restrictions. But even 57,178 coyotes is a lot of coyotes. The greatest yearly total ever taken was 111,076 in 1942, just before the coming of compound 1080.

The coyote is adaptable enough to prosper in this alpine environment.

There are lots of coyotes.

They are widespread, traveling north, west, south down the narrowing part of Mexico on their own four feet, and carried into the urban areas of the east by people who took coyote pups home as pets. These folks found that coyotes made poor pets when grown, and released them. Other coyotes were actually introduced into the east to provide a good substitute for the red fox, the focal point of the hound chase for the "yoicks and tallyho" set.

Weep not for the "pore lil' Ole Coyote." He is as numerous in the 1980s as he ever was. His home range is greater than it ever was. He has learned to live with human beings very well.

Chapter 5

The First Year of a Coyote

The first thing Blackfoot knew was the warmth of five other baby coyotes crowded against him in the darkness of the den. Their mother had modified an old badger burrow for a place to give birth. In fact, she cleaned out six other dens before coming to this one. The six pups were round, fat, short-legged, full of curiosity, and covered with fleas. Some of the fleas came from their mother who suffered from the coyotes' universal pest, but others were already in the den, perhaps from another coyote.

The pups were identical, except that this one male had a black front right paw. In all other respects, the pups were healthy copies of each other. They were born April 12, in New Mexico's Hidalgo County, and the parent coyotes found it easy to feed their young brood on abundant rodents and quail nests. For the first two weeks of their life all food was in the form of mother's milk, but at the end of their second week, the bitch came into the burrow with a stomach full of quail eggs and mice—regurgitating them into the big end of the burrow. The pups were confused at first, but sniffed at the semi-crushed eggs, licked and then greedily ate them, shells and all. The mice took a bit longer to get used to, but soon all the pups were filling up greedily on the food that was daily regurgitated into the den. Nevertheless, they still battled for preferred positions when their mother nursed them.

Three weeks old, Blackfoot led a reconnaisance of the den tunnel

21

with his siblings. They looked up at the circle of light that their mother came through when entering the den. Blackfoot led the way, climbing up the sloping tunnel to the dazzling bright of the sunlit world. Climbing over each other's backs and wrestling for the best position, the pups took turns staring out at the green grass, the blue sky, and the big white clouds floating overhead.

For the better part of two days they went up and down the tunnel, stealing good looks at the world, then tumbling back into the safer feeling darkness of the den. But in the den the pups spent most of their time scratching and biting at the fleas which now made life truly miserable below ground. The next morning, Blackfoot actually went above ground!

It all happened quite innocently—for he never really intended to come all the way out. A horned lark was singing not fifteen feet from the burrow, and Blackfoot had stretched his neck to see the source of the song. When the bird moved to a lower spot, the pup stretched to see where it had gone and actually tumbled over himself. There he was . . . standing in the sunlight, out of the den! He moved to investigate the western horned lark, but it flew. Sur-

Blackfoot peers out of the den, getting his first good look at the sunlit world.

22

prised, he tried to run after the bird, but tripped over his big puppy feet and fell. Blackfoot liked being outside. Before he could scamper back to the burrow, the other pups were all out, looking at Blackfoot with new-found admiration; for he was now the leader. He was first in everything, including feeling the sharp teeth and the irritated growl of his mother who suddenly appeared out of nowhere to throw the too-brave pups back into the den. This time the bitch did not go into the burrow with the pups, but laid down outside of the tunnel. Her sharp growl sent the pups below if they tried to stick their noses out. She brought no food that day, nor did she allow them to nurse. When the male coyote came to the den at sunset, he regurgitated a dozen mice and parts of a road-killed jackrabbit onto the hard-packed dirt. The female snapped up one choice morsel for herself, then allowed the pups to come out for dinner.

When it was fully dark, the bitch picked up one of the pups in her mouth and disappeared. She was gone about fifteen minutes, then returned to repeat the process with a second pup. When the male came close to the pups, she sent him scuttling away in surprise with a snarling, biting approach. He tucked his tail between his legs and went off on his nocturnal hunt. By midnight she had moved all six pups to a new burrow, another cleaned-out badger hole.

Satisfied with the family's new home, the bitch trotted two hundred yards south of the new den, then pointed her nose to the sky and howled, a long quavering call into the emptiness of the night. From a quarter mile to the westward the answer came, and she trotted off to join her mate in the serious business of hunting. The pups were excited and nervous in their new home, but appreciated that it was relatively free of fleas. They luxuriated in the dustbathing it provided, inside the wide main entrance.

Twice during the night the parents came to the new den, regurgitated food for the pups and disappeared. Sunrise found the father in a shadowy recess beneath an outcropping of sandstone, curled up and sound asleep. The mother was about one hundred yards downwind of the den, half in and half out of a caved-in badger hole under a pack rat nest. Her sensitive nose helped her keep track of the young during the sunlit hours, while she stayed well away. This was the first night that she hadn't allowed the pups to nurse at all, and they had spent wakeful hours gnawing at old bones in the den entrance.

By the beginning of July the sun shone down relentlessly,

scorching the gravelly soil with its burning rays, driving the last bit of moisture out of grass and animal alike. The pups, nearing their adult size now, were suffering from dehydration, and the den became a noxious place with the results of diarrhea.

One evening, just as it was getting dark, the bitch returned to the den and called the pups outside. When they tried to nurse, she snapped at them with a new sharpness. Puzzled and worried, the pups kept away, not sure where they stood in this new order of things. But as she turned to leave, the bitch's attitude invited the pups to follow and they did, loping along, clumsily and noisily after her.

The mother's first stop was at a *pila,* as the Spanish-speaking cowboys called the water tank that was fed by a windmill-operated pump. When they first encountered water, standing in the tracks of cattle near the *pila,* they splashed in it, then attempted to bite it. It tasted good! They continued to lick and bite it into chunks until they saw the bitch put her front paws up on the edge of the water tank and lower her head to drink in the tank itself, where the water was cleaner. The pups promptly followed suit and drank so much water that they almost foundered themselves. When the bitch started out on the hunt, the pups carried bulging bellies through their world of sage and creosote bush, bitterbrush, and stunted prickly pear.

That night the pups learned to hunt for mice, an occupation which would take up much of their waking hours for the rest of their lives. They watched the mother coyote as she moved forward very slowly, head cocked to one side as she listened for sounds of mice moving under the bunches of bent grass. When she heard a mouse, her head came down to the level of the grass tops and her delicate hearing instrument determined the exact location. Then she sprang, front feet and head high in the air, and came down with her front feet on top of the mouse. Sometimes she judged it exactly and pinned the mouse to the ground long enough to grab it with her long canine teeth and pull it out of the grass concealment. Other times the mouse darted out from under her paws. She would grab for it in the grass as it ran for safety. Very few mice eluded her, not after she pinpointed their location.

Excited and hungry, the pups tried to take the mice away from their mother—just once—and were met by a growl and snapping teeth that told them they were all done freeloading and would have to do most of their own hunting from now on. One of the pups grabbed a scurrying mouse that had escaped his mother momentarily. He snapped it up triumphantly, crunched it once and swallowed it. When the mother's jaws snapped shut beside his ear, the pup growled sharply and she moved away. He was now a hunter on his own right, having made his first real kill.

Blackfoot was not the quickest learner of the group. He didn't make his first mouse kill until the mother coyote carried a mouse in her mouth, dropped it in front of him and let him grab it as it tried to scurry away. As the first graying appeared in the east, the six pups were spread out across the meadow, all hunting diligently. They never returned to the den. The daylight hours were spent lying in the warm shade of a creosote bush, across ten acres, all half asleep, half awake—the normal condition for a healthy coyote.

By late August the pups were expert mouse hunters and even cooperated in a few unsuccessful attempts to run down blacktailed jackrabbits. Blackfoot distinguished himself by nabbing a cottontail rabbit that was a bit slow in diving for its den when the hunting pack appeared. The coyotes still foraged as a unit, although the male parent seldom came along. Every three or four days as they started their rounds, he would appear and approach the bitch slowly and carefully. The male and female would go through an elaborate ritual of touching noses, rubbing sides, and smelling each other before starting out with the pups. But before they got used to the idea of hunting with the father, he would disappear—probably repelled by their clumsiness.

On one of the father coyote's rare appearances, the next exciting thing happened. In broad daylight, about nine o'clock in the morning, a stranger coyote suddenly walked across their valley! The bitch jumped to her feet, stared intently, then ran toward the stranger. Halfway to the newcomer, who had stopped and turned its side to them, back humped and tail tucked between its legs in the submissive posture, the female stopped and started to howl. She was immediately joined by the male, who howled several times in concert with her, then ran toward the intruder. The pups gamboled along behind, excited by their parents' behavior and curious about the stranger. They never got a chance to get acquainted, however, for the male coyote suddenly drove in against the newcomer, bumping it with his chest and knocking it on its back. There it wriggled in submission, swinging its tail from side to side like a happy dog, and baring its teeth—not in a menacing biting gesture, but in a rather foolish looking, "grinning" gesture of complete submission. The male parent walked around it stiff-

25

legged, smelling its inguinal region while it wriggled its message, "Don't hurt me—I'm no danger to anyone!"

The stranger was a young male, and neither of the resident pair wanted anything to do with him. The bitch took the initiative, diving in and snapping a few bites at the stranger's unprotected flanks. He whirled and took off at high speed, with both adults after him. They chased him for a quarter of a mile. It was obvious that they were not trying to catch the intruder, but simply escort him out of their domain. When he crossed the invisible boundary limit of their territory toward the rugged Hatchet Mountains, the pursuit stopped.

For fifteen minutes the adult pair howled a group song, which the pups tried to join. In between howls, the male walked stiff-legged to a creosote bush beside the trail, urinated, and scratched long rips in the sandy soil to mark his territory. The female watched for a while, then trotted back toward the daytime lay up area.

The incident had not been without danger to the coyote family. Two young men from Albuquerque had heard the prolonged coyote howling session. They were in the area on a scouting trip, looking for a good place to go hunting that fall. Both had permits for the limited javelina season and were looking for the diminutive porkers and the small-but-regal Coues whitetailed deer they would seek in a few months. Three hours after the howling concert, the two men walked quietly into the creosote brush from the truck parked beside State Road #81. Each man carried a rifle, and one held a strange looking call, modified from a duck call. They found a short knoll and quickly secreted themselves on it, sitting quietly back to back to keep a sharp look out around the compass.

After a ten minute wait, one of the men put the call up to his mouth and blew it. The yelping, quavering scream of pain rang unnaturally loud on the ears of the coyote family, for the caller was inept. But the young coyotes hadn't yet learned to be cautious. Four of them dashed directly toward the sound. The adult pair reacted differently. The male, who had lost two mates to the predator call and rifle, hesitated only a second, then ran swiftly away from the call. Blackfoot happened to be near him, so he followed his father out of habit. The mother coyote slunk out of her daytime bed and began a slow circle to get downwind of the noisy invitation to dinner.

The four pups ran clumsily toward the two hunters. They stopped in foolish amazement when the two men suddenly materi-

26

alized in front of them—and stared. Two shots rang out and two of them were slammed to the ground, dead before they hit. The other two, terrified by the sound of the rifles, did an about face and ran for their lives. The two men fired a total of seven more shots, but only one hit. It ripped through the gut of the smallest female pup just as she tried to jump over a dried prickly pear cactus. She whined once in pain, turned to pull herself free of the cactus and fell dead as a second shot ripped through her chest.

None of the coyotes took notice that only three pups followed their mother on the hunt now. They purposefully avoided the spot where the men had hidden, and where the pups had died, not from any feeling of emotion, but simply because the man smell lingered—and they found it unpleasant.

In September, dovehunters invaded the coyotes' land, walking through the dry brushlands in search of the fast-flying grey ghosts of the bird world. Shotgun pellets tore into another one of the pups as it fled from a hunter who had blundered into its noonday rest. The hunter said, "Guess I missed it. Didn't even draw a yip out of that coyote!" But he was wrong. Seven of the #6 pellets had ripped into the coyote, puncturing intestines and causing internal bleeding of the liver. The pup took three days to die. The father found the bloating body two days later and ate part of it. Black buzzards found the remainder at first light and quickly removed all the flesh from the pup—leaving only clean bones and the torn hide under the creosote bush.

Young scaled quail were everywhere now, and nighttime hunting was easy. The quail roosted on the ground, or on the low branches of the brush, and the coyote trio simply had to use their nose until they located the birds, sneak in quietly from three sides, and then pounce. They usually got one apiece. There were now only three mouths to feed, for the male was nowhere to be seen. Blackfoot and a young female worked closely with their mother and became an efficient hunting team. They learned how to take turns running a blacktailed jackrabbit until the rabbit tired, and then pushed it close to another of the trio lying in wait. Even when the trio cooperated in the hunt for a rabbit, they still fought over the meal. There was much teeth snapping and warning growls before the rabbit carcass was cleaned up.

The months of late fall were easy for the trio. Blackfoot spent many an hour catching grasshoppers in the early morn before they were warmed up enough to jump very far. Between grasshoppers and a never ending supply of small meadow mice, life was pleasant.

Add to that great numbers of scaled quail, a few blue quail, and lots of very small cottontail rabbits—Blackfoot couldn't ask for more.

Blackfoot's greatest adventure during this period was a failed attempt to kill a young javelina shoat that had wandered away from its mother. A herd of fifteen javelina grazed on *lecheguilla* and prickly pear cactus across the flats stretching up to the Hatchet Mountains and Blackfoot's territory. Blackfoot made a quick run after the distracted tiny pig, caught it by the hind leg, and spun it to the ground. Instead of driving for the neck hold, as his mother would have done, Blackfoot put a big front paw on the tiny pig, which terrified, promptly sent up a piercing scream. Surprised and somewhat disconcerted by the shrill scream, and amazed at the volume of sound that poured from the puny porker, Blackfoot almost didn't move quickly enough to avoid the four adult javelinas that bounded to the shoat's rescue. Snorting angrily with every hair standing on end and the air filling with the musk scent of danger, the five big pigs popped their jaws with a machine gun sound. Their grunts were definitely not friendly. Knocked off balance by the first pig, which drove straight into him, Blackfoot scrambled to his feet, dodged the second one, and ran as fast as he could to get away from the other three very determined pigs.

The chase continued for three hundred yards, but Blackfoot drew steadily away and the pigs gave it up as a bad job. With his tail still tucked up between his legs, Blackfoot looked back at the scene and decided that javelinas, like rattlesnakes, were not to be tampered with. The rattlesnake lesson had come in the form of a painful nip from his mother when he started to investigate the strange smelling big snake curled up under a dried up cholla plant. She added second nip as he scuttled for safety, just for emphasis.

By late December Blackfoot and his father were almost identical in size. They looked exactly the same with the same coloration, except for the black foot. Gradually the young coyotes grew apart from their mother; the father was never seen, although Blackfoot came across his scent posts at times. When he did, Blackfoot found himself walking stiff-legged around the scent post, sniffing it carefully, then adding his own urine to the marker of the family's domain.

In January the year's only snowstorm gave Blackfoot more excitement. For half an hour strong winds blew big wet snowflakes horizontally—the air was full of soft, white wetness that melted upon hitting the ground and left pretty patterns of white and gray

By the time he was ten months old, Blackfoot was hard to tell from his parents at a distance.

across the creosote bush. Blackfoot ran into the wind, jumping to catch individual snowflakes, and licking his nose in surprise when it collided with a few drops of cold water. He sniffed the snowflakes as they hit the ground, and looked at the wet spot in surprise which had just been a snowflake. Half an hour later, the sun shone brightly and the snow was soon forgotten.

During the second week of February, Blackfoot came upon his mother and sister hunting together. He was attracted to the two by their howling as they started on the evening hunt. Another surprise was in store after his sister and mother both met him with the usual ceremonial sniffs and shoulder bumps. As he exchanged investigative sniffs with his sister, the father coyote came flying out of the brush with a menacing growl and bumped Blackfoot with his chest, knocking him to the ground. The pup promptly turned submissive, rolling abjectly on his back, grinning to show that he meant no harm, but the older coyote was not in a forgiving mood and promptly drove him away with a few severe bites on the hindquarters.

Blackfoot couldn't explain the sudden antagonism shown by his father, but somehow, dimly, he felt that it was connected with the strange and exciting new odor that came from both his mother and the young female. Blackfoot hung back, sniffing the air with great intensity, trying to locate that wonderful odor again. After two hours he drifted off into the brush, driven by hunger. Blackfoot spent a lonely night mousing. Later he found his favorite den spot, where he could lay up out of sight, and still have the warm sun on his back during most of the day.

Life was easy now. Blackfoot could fill his belly with an hour's hunting almost any time of the night and day; so he spent much of his time just investigating the sights and sounds of the ten square mile territory which seemed to be home to his family group. Often he went to the edge of the territory, found the markers to be sure, then set up his lonesome quavering howl. When a strange coyote howled from far off in the distance, Blackfoot felt strangely excited. He wanted to investigate, but was afraid to leave the friendly boundaries of his own home.

Excitement conquered his fear of the unknown one night and he went farther north than he had ever been, howling and moving closer to the sounds of the answering howls from another coyote. Finally he came upon three strangers—shadowy forms in the moonlight, standing and watching as he approached. He came up in typical submissive posture, doing everything but lying down and rolling over to show that he was friendly. Then he smelled it again, that wonderful attracting smell that had come from both his mother and his sister last week—the smell of a female coyote in heat.

Two of the three coyotes were females and met Blackfoot with cautious investigative sniffing and tentative touching; the third coyote was a male, about the same age as Blackfoot and slightly smaller. He came up stiff-legged and snarling, eager to show that he was the boss. Blackfoot surprised himself by meeting him with ears laid back and lips raised to expose his teeth in a threatening gesture. They circled each other warily a few times, then the male turned away to return to the smallest of the females.

The other female coyote sniffed noses with Blackfoot again, then scampered around in a circle like a playful puppie dog. Excited and eager, he chased her and followed when she led him off into the sagebrush. There she let Blackfoot catch up to her and they trotted side by side for half an hour, moving along the invisible but very real boundary of the scent-posted boundary between the two family territories. They did a little tentative mousing, but Blackfoot couldn't concentrate on the mice with that overpoweringly attractive smell in his nose.

Just before daylight he was walking slowly behind her with his nose almost touching her tail, which she carried up and to one side, instead of dragging as it usually did. She turned and snapped her teeth within half an inch of his nose, then circled around to stand directly alongside of him. She pressed her body against his and gave him a strong bump, almost a shove, with her front shoulders; then moved past him to stand in front.

After sniffing her inguinal region again, he whined in excitement and mounted her. They coupled immediately. Their amorous activity lasted only four or five minutes. As he tried to slip off of her, part of him seemed to be caught in her genitals. He hopped clumsily, trying to walk on his back feet as she tried to move out from under him. The copulatory tie only lasted for another five minutes. Once free he promptly sat down and started licking his genitals, while she trotted about fifty feet away and did the same.

For the next three days the two stayed together, never more than twenty feet apart, and mated again and again. When that deliciously wonderful smell was gone they became a hunting pair. The coyotes moved together in perfect rhythm on the hunt, cooperating as if they were one mind directing two bodies in the search for rabbits, quail, ground squirrels, garter snakes, and the ever-present, ever-important field mouse that made up a large part of their diet.

Now they howled together to announce the coming of twilight, and when they heard an answering howl, they barked and howled and moved closer to it—then stopped and marked their boundary with scent spots and much scratching of dirt backward with their hind feet. They always howled in unison now, and the answering sounds weren't familiar at all. They were staking out their own hunting territory and getting ready for the next chapter of the story, when Blackfoot's mate began to clean out dens, preparing to give birth to her own pups.

Although she was nervous and irritable and often drove him away when he tried to investigate the den she was cleaning out, Blackfoot's mate always followed him on the hunts and gladly accepted the mice he brought to her from time to time. Blackfoot was now a full grown coyote who was lucky enough to have found a mate in his first full year. The cycle was complete. The new pair looked forward to their next year on their own territory.

Chapter 6

The Coyote in 1492

How many coyotes abounded in America when Columbus discovered our great land? Where did these animals live when the first Europeans landed on these shores?

There is a temptation to say that the coyote was found only in a circumscribed niche in the western plains: west of the forested lands of Missouri, Arkansas, Louisiana, Minnesota and Iowa; east of the Pacific coastal ranges; south of what is now the Canadian border; and, north of middle Mexico.

Yes, there is a temptation to say that the coyote occupied only this one fifth of the North American continent—but there are some facts which argue for a much larger distribution area and home range that cannot be ignored. For example, the Aztecs named the animal *coyotl;* the Aztecs live south of that middle of Mexico marker. The coyote must have lived all through the land of the Aztec—including far south of middle Mexico. Some scientists suggest that the Aztecs came from Asia over the land bridge and might have tarried long enough in the prime coyote country of the Great Plains to pick up the name for this animal. I don't buy that. I think the coyote lived way south of the United States—perhaps as far south as Costa Rica.

The coyote is found in the mythology of most Indian tribes, from the Athabaskan and Cree of northern Canada to the Sioux and Ojibway of the plains, to the Tarahumara, Yaqui, Zapotec, and

Mixtec of southern Mexico. His likeness is found on clay pottery excavated from the earliest known Mexican ruins, which pre-dates ruins found in the portion of the continent now occupied by the lower forty-eight.

Recent studies in Alaska and northern Canada raise doubts that the coyote is a newcomer to that cold country. These studies suggest that the coyote was always present, but in very small numbers. I can agree with that theory.

It seems doubtful that there were coyotes in the southeastern United States back in 1492. That ecological niche was occupied by two larger canine predators, the timber wolf and the red wolf. The same argument can be made for the Maritime Provinces, Ontario and Manitoba and the northeastern quarter of the United States, which are the best ranges of the larger timber wolf.

With the possible exception of the badger, the coyote has no friends outside of his immediate subspecies.

Consider the situation for the coyote in 1492. He was hunted down, killed, and eaten by his larger cousin the timber wolf. This is still true in the wolf country of Alaska and the Yukon. A coyote has little chance of living long in territory cruised by a hunting pack of true wolves. The larger, stronger, faster, more enduring wolf has little trouble running down and no trouble killing the coyote. No lobo or timber wolf will allow a coyote to come near it, much less share its kill. Coyotes have been observed following the large wolves and (supposedly) feeding from their kills after the wolf has sated his appetite. After having seen a few wolf kills, however, it is my opinion that the coyote would have a hard time finding a meal from wolf leftovers.

Way back in the late 1920s to early 1940s, a large grey wolf terrorized ranchers and sheepmen in western South Dakota near the town of Custer. He was reputed to cause losses in excess of $25,000—when a prime steer sold for forty to fifty bucks. This wolf also killed horses, and seemed to be possessed of a devilish cunning that enabled him to elude the most skilled trappers and poisoners during that period. The famous Custer Wolf was reputed to have two coyotes patrolling its flanks, feeding on its kills after the wolf left. Certainly, even then, there was no friendship or symbiotic relationship, other than what the coyote forced upon the wolf.

In times of winter starvation, puma have been known to catch and kill coyotes—and to eat the bodies. This is by no means a usual happening, but has been reported often enough to be believed.

Bears will also eat coyotes, even the ones that already have been destroyed by our anti-coyote programs. This is no surprise to anyone who knows the rather universal tastes of the bear, who will eat anything that doesn't bite him first—no matter how odorous, fetid, rotted, or unappetizing it may become. My personal belief, however, is that the bear, lacking speed and agility, does not habitually prey on the coyote.

We begin to get the picture of a plains dwelling animal whose range was bounded by forested lands to the east, which it did not like to enter. The forests held enemies such as the wolf and red wolf, both too strong and swift for the coyote to compete with on an even basis. On the Great Plains, there was a constant source of carrion food, provided by the remains of bison, elk (originally a plains animal before mankind drove it into the mountains), antelope, and mule deer. In the summer Prairie Dogs, whose towns stretched for endless miles over the plains provided a never-ending food supply. This was an area which allowed the careful, canny coyote to see his wolf enemy long before it saw him. It was possible for the coyote to stay away from the wolf—and he did so.

Migratory waterfowl nested in great abundance through the summer months in the northern half of coyoteland. In the southern half of that same coyote range, waterfowl wintered in tremendous flocks, providing winter food for thousands of coyotes. Even today, coyotes patrol the edges of the wintering goose flocks on the Bosque del Apache National Wildlife Refuge here in my home state of New Mexico, and pick off the occasional sick or aged goose which has lost its native caution or is unable to fly. Apparently, these coyotes do not increase mortality of the wintering geese, but simply act as scavengers to clean up the birds which would have died anyway.

A different situation is found on the nesting ground, where the birds are exceptionally vulnerable. At northern waterfowl areas such as the Lower Souris National Wildlife Refuge in North Dakota the coyote is a significant force in reducing production. The coyote may also be affecting the Canadian duck and goose producing areas.

The coyote was much smarter than the larger wolf, demonstrated by his greater ability to survive mankind's assaults. As the wolf was extirpated from great parts of his former domain, the coyote increased its numbers to fill the vacant niche. The coyote was soon common in areas where it had been unknown. As the red wolf proved unable to cope with mankind, the coyote took over its

35

range and diluted the gene pool by inter-breeding with the larger red wolf.

Wildlife managers often point with pride to the fact that there are many times as many whitetailed deer in America than there were when Columbus arrived. The whitetail is a creature of edge habitat, and mankind's croplands, interspersed with native woodlands, has offered such improved *lebensraum* for the deer, whose population has exploded. There are now probably more whitetailed deer in Texas than there were in the entire North American continent five hundred years ago.

Today, there are certainly more coyotes in North America—by a factor of ten to one—than there were in 1492. This tremendous increase has been due to many factors such as the disappearance of the coyotes' fatal enemy, the timber wolf, and the great adaptability of the coyote to move into a new habitat as the opportunity presents itself. The ultimate opportunist, the coyote is far more numerous than he was in centuries past. And man is responsible.

Chapter 7

Never the Expected

Near the Willow Beach National Fish Hatchery on the Colorado River between Arizona and Nevada, we used the big fish barge to stock rainbow trout into the cool waters beneath the warm surface waters. The Colorado river has quite a bit of current left, at this point, before diving under the stationary lake water. The river was perhaps three hundred yards wide in this particular spot.

We started for the hatchery after freeing millions of three inch trout into the cool water. It was late June, and the temperature must have been over 110°F. I squatted down to get in the scant shade of the big tank on our barge to protect my camera bag and my tender skin from the direct sun. I then saw the coyote.

The coyote was swimming strongly toward the Arizona shore, on a course which would collide with ours if we both held course and speed. I called the helmsman's attention to the coyote, but he didn't seem at all surprised. At my request we slowed slightly to come up alongside the coyote. Head up and alert, he watched us approach, but did not turn back, in fact he made no attempt to escape from the big boat. As we came directly alongside, he turned to swim around the barge and continue his path to the Arizona shore. We maneuvered to stay in front of him and foil his crossing attempt. He tried several times to go around us. Failing that, he simply waited for us to tire of the game.

His only concession to normal coyote behavior was to stay out of reach of any club that might have been swung from the barge. He did not even consider the possibility of returning to the Nevada side, but rather waited till we tired of interposing ourselves between him and his goal. When we moved out of his way, he swam strongly to the Arizona side, climbed out and shook himself like a wet dog, then trotted up the rocky bank without a backward glance at the three men on the fish-planting barge.

Even coyotes raised in deserts seem to be strong swimmers. Yet most coyotes fear man and avoid him with every fiber of their being. This one had other, more important things to do, such as crossing a river. Why? Probably, as the hatchery man said, the coyote wanted to get to the other side.

After a coyote hunting expedition that featured the successful use of a predator call, I slowly drove down a seldom used New Mexico side road. I saw a coyote stand up from his bedding spot beside a big prickly pear cactus. I eased out of the car and tried an offhand shot at the coyote, two hundred yards away. I missed. At the blast of the gun, the coyote jumped about four feet off the ground, spun around and high-tailed it over the ridge and out of sight before I could fire another salute at his disappearing posterior. Normal behavior? Absolutely. He must have been a little sleepy, though, to have let me have the first futile shot. I took the cartridge shell out of the barrel, climbed back in the car, and headed for home.

I had gone less than one hundred feet when the coyote (I can only assume that it was the same one) came trotting over the ridge towards me! I piled out in a hurry, jacked a bullet into the gun, and fired a second shot at the coyote. Again I missed, but this time I had an excuse of sorts, for the coyote was in the process of flipping into reverse and high-tailing it out of there a second time. Now, I figured that this coyote was just slightly forgetful; as it had plumb forgotten that there was a human being with a rifle over there. . . . Can you think of another reason?

But wait, the story goes on. I took my rifle and walked quietly toward the ridge, hoping that he had stopped his flight and was waiting for me to leave the vicinity. Slipping just my eyeballs over the ridge, I carefully looked for any sign of the coyote. I slowly inched higher and higher until I finally could see all the valley below. No coyote in sight. Topping out, I carefully glassed every inch of the valley, no coyote. Knowing that I might well have been looking right at him without seeing him, I shouldered the rifle and started back toward the scene of the original encounter—

simply because it offered better footing and a better route to the road.

Suddenly the coyote popped up in front of me, not more than forty feet away! He had evidently returned to his bed and was probably just dozing off when I flushed him again. In fact, he must have been asleep. He stopped for a second to look back at me— from a range of fifty or sixty yards. That time I didn't miss. Close examination showed that there was nothing physically wrong with the animal. Its lack of caution couldn't be attributed to youth. This was a full grown adult coyote—in a heavily hunted area.

Explanation? Beats me.

My wife's folks lived on a farm near the Pipestem River in Stutsman County, North Dakota. On a very cold January morning when the sun tried hard to warm a solid blanket of snow that stretched to the horizon, I heard a lot of yapping outside the house. Looking out a side window of the house, I saw that the farmstead dog, a rather small Heinz 57, was barking at a coyote standing silently about two hundred yards out to the west, in the direction of the Pipestem. I went to the back door and said, "Sic 'em!" to the small dog. That bolstered the nerve of the ten pound bundle of domesticated canine and he went rushing—a bold frontal attack— at the coyote. That twenty pound bundle of wild canine turned and fled, effortlessly running over the drifted snow toward the river. The dog seemed to be gaining on the coyote as they went out of sight.

Suddenly the excited chase-barking of the dog turned to a pan-icky yipping of fright, and the two came running back toward the buildings, the coyote almost, but not quite, catching up to the frightened dog. When the dog got to about within one hundred yards of the buildings, the coyote slowed and stopped. He then sat down and watched the dog fleeing for his life.

I opened the back door an inch and spoke to the dog. "What's the matter, fella, scared of that little coyote?" Hearing my voice, the dog regained his courage and again charged the coyote. This time the coyote tried to call its bluff by holding his ground until the dog was within fifteen feet. The coyote then whirled and took off with the dog nipping at his heels. At the edge of the hill the coyote turned and aimed for the dog in deadly earnest. This time the coyote had murder on his mind! The dog did some really fancy evasive running, "ki-yi-ing" at the top of his voice, and scooted for the safety of the buildings again. The coyote came to within one hundred feet of the house, turned and disappeared over the hill.

The dog's behavior is easily explained—every dog is brave in its own yard, especially with its pet human watching. But how do you explain the coyote's uncharacteristic actions?

Was the coyote playing a game with the dog? Or was he deadly serious, luring the dog away from the safety of the buildings, into the dangers of the wild? What did the coyote have in mind? Was he figuring on dining on that dog? Seems unlikely. Even in winter there was no shortage of mice and rabbits for the coyote to eat, and he certainly seemed to be in good condition. I do not pretend to understand the coyote psyche and can offer no explanation.

If you want to outwit the coyote, prepare for the unexpected. He can show you animal genius, and he can be the biggest boob in the wild. But don't count on any favors. Don't even count on coyotes doing the unpredictable.

Chapter 8

The Bounty System

To encourage the hunting and killing of a certain wildlife species, just put a price on its head. Say that you will pay a bounty—say four dollars—for every coyote killed and presented to the county official. Surely that will attract more coyote hunters and trappers, who will kill more coyotes. Logic follows that we will have fewer coyotes and fewer economic losses by coyotes.

Sorry, it doesn't work that way.

Responsible wildlife technicians have known for almost a hundred years that bounties do not work—though many states continue to pay these bounties. Many state game and fish departments have eliminated predator bounties, only to have the state legislature restore them as soon as the session began. Why do we pay bounties? Primarily because the very few who benefit from receiving these cash payments form a very vocal group that fools legislators into thinking they are doing something to help populations of livestock or wild game. The second reason is simply tradition. We always have paid bounties so we will continue to pay bounties.

We recognized the wastefulness of the bounty system many years ago. Few have stated it as eloquently as Gerald E. Eddy, Director of the Michigan Department of Conservation, usually ranked as one of the nation's most progressive departments. . . . "We waste almost one quarter million dollars per year on a worthless project—bounties. One quarter of a million dollars per year—license fees from 80,000 hunters—almost three and a half million dollars since 1935. Three and a half million dollars would have bought up a lot of good public hunting land, a lot of good duck hunting marsh like Pointe Mouillee south of Detroit, and a lot of public fishing sites for fishermen and boater access to water. It could have built thirty duck hunting and fishing projects like the big Martiny flooding in Mecosta County. It could have been used to teach thousands of our kids about our land, water and wildlife that we all love and want them to enjoy. These are permanent benefits. We could have done these things, and a lot more, but we didn't. We poured the three and a half million dollars down a rathole. Every conservation official in North America will tell you that bounties are a flagrant waste of sportsmen's money. Hunters aren't getting what they are paying for. . . . " Mr. Eddy wrote these words way back in 1963.

Let's read on a bit farther, as Mr. Eddy wrote, "But bounties failed to control predators . . . 4,328 coyotes bountied in 1961, an all time high . . . and in spite of these record high bounty payments, there are more and more foxes, coyotes and Upper Peninsula bobcats being killed!"

The late Roger Latham, with a doctorate in wildlife management, was one of the most respected outdoor writers. As outdoor editor of the Pittsburgh Free Press, chief of Wildlife Research for the Pennsylvania Game Department, and author of the most authoritative book written about wild turkeys, Dr. Latham built a reputation for honesty and for keen insight into wildlife problems. Let's listen to what he said in 1960:

"The science of wildlife management has come of age and barbershop biology is rapidly being replaced by true wildlife biology."

"You say, if this is true, why are bounties still being paid in 33 states? The answer is tradition which can be overcome only through a long educational program, no matter how convincing the facts."

"William Penn started the bounty business in this country way back in 1683 by paying for the scalps of wolves. These large animals were destroying the livestock of his people living in Penn's Woods. The bounty spread to mountain lions, bobcats, lynx, coyotes, bears and other large predators—all destroyers of man's domestic animals."

"In Pennsylvania, where rewards for fox scalps have been paid

A. B. Bynum and wife Alanson, on trapline with one day's catch of coyote scalps. There have been many successful husband and wife combos on the trapline.

off and on since 1717, and constantly since 1907, these animals have been at an all time high for the last 15 years. . . . In fact, the annual harvest of foxes in most states is no greater than it is for many game animals which are being carefully fostered and protected."

During the five hundred years during which the European sub-species of *Homo sapiens* has severely damaged the wildlife resources of North America, millions of dollars in bounties have been paid. Unless you ascribe to it some value as a source of income for farm boys, pool hall loafers, and those who illegally bounty animals they pick up off the road, this money has been wasted. The greatest folly of all was when Alaska paid a bounty on Dolly Varden trout trails, on the basis that the trout ate the spawn of salmon. The trout had actually been eating the spawn of salmon for millions of years without hurting the salmon population.

No state or province has reduced predatory animal population by paying a bounty! Not one! Not anywhere! Yet, we still pay bounties. We learn slowly.

How slowly? Well, in 1958 an official of the Ontario government said, "Ninety eight years of consecutive bounty payments in Ontario has not reduced the population of either the timber wolf or the brush wolf (coyote)." Minnesota paid out $1.5 million in bounties in the dozen years up to 1956. Did the payment of all this money reduce the numbers of coyotes in Minnesota? Not according to the toll of coyotes bountied per year as follows:

1953.	2,352	coyotes
1954.	1,490	"
1955.	2,144	"
1956.	1,751	"
1957.	1,726	"

It is quite possible that many of the coyotes bountied in Minnesota in the 1950s were killed in North Dakota. Minnesota offered a top dollar for bounty hunters, twenty-five bucks per coyote; North Dakota paid only five dollars. It has been proven that Missouri and Kansas both paid out bounties for North Dakota coyotes, which had been transported south for the higher bounty payment.

Don Balser, who had a long and distinguished career with the U.S. Fish and Wildlife Service after working for the Minnesota Department, summed up the problems of the bounty system way back in 1958, in Minnesota's Informational Leaflet No. 1:

(1) Too few predators are bountied to bring about reduction of the breeding stock, so that the whole population can be reduced.

(2) The bounty system results in unnecessary payments—payments are being made for predators that would have been killed anyway, without the bounty.

(3) The bounty system is a shotgun approach, aimed at an entire species across an entire state, and does not get at the animal causing the economic loss.

(4) Bounty systems are invitations to fraud. House cats are bountied as bobcats, dogs as coyotes or wolves . . . and scalps are transported from low-pay to high-pay states.

(5) The bounty system encourages "farming" of predators. Some trappers bounty the males and the pups, letting the female go free to produce more bounty-eligible animals for next year. . . .

(8) **There is no proof that bountying of predators has increased the harvest of game animals in Minnesota or elsewhere.**

North Dakotans have been very adept at transporting their coyote pelts to states paying a higher bounty. When South Dakota paid twice as much as North Dakota, it was interesting to compare total numbers tallied by identical size counties on both sides of that imaginary line. South Dakotans paid for North Dakota coyotes.

North Dakota began paying a state bounty on coyotes in 1898; that year 5,520 coyotes were bountied. After 45 years, the number of coyotes bountied in 1943 was 5,701, about the same. But in 1946 the number went up to 11,867! Surely the bounty had not served its purpose of lowering the number of coyotes. The increased numbers bountied in 1946 reflect both the availability of many coyotes and the fact that bounty hunters in North Dakota were much more efficient at killing coyotes with aerial tactics. Also, there was a great increase in numbers of young men trained in the use of firearms—primarily young veterans of World War II. But the fact is that the bounty had not cut down on North Dakota's coyote population, not after 48 years of operation.

In 1960, 33 states were still paying bounties. Yes, we do learn very slowly. Will putting a thirty dollar price on the coyotes head cause its numbers to be reduced? Of course not.

Nature is very wasteful at times. She plans very extravagantly, allowing a single female fish to produce millions of eggs. Nature always produces a surplus of coyotes, as she produces a surplus of quail, or pheasants, or mule deer. Part of that surplus of quail and pheasants and deer is harvested by the biggest predator of all, man. The bounty paid for coyotes induces man to take some of the surplus population, but without any appreciable effect upon the population of coyotes.

Yes, we learn slowly. Does your state still pay a bounty? If so, are you happy about this waste of your money?

The Navajo Indians refer to the coyote as "Little Brother," but not when it is depredating upon their sheep flocks, which are the main source of food and income for the Navajo. Here the sheep are foraging on the sparse vegetation of the desert portions of the big Navajo reservation in Arizona.

Chapter 9

Coyotes and Indians

Coyotes play an important part in American Indian mythology. In some cultures they take the part of a benevolent, semi-divine spirit; in others they become the devil incarnate. Some believe the name "coyote" was the Spanish adaptation of the Nahuatl word "coyotl." He is called "little Brother" by the Navajo and the Apache. Many Indian cultures carved the coyote head onto human figures; and some cultures even have specific "coyote" dances.

The Navajo (whose name means "The People") are the most numerous of the Indian tribes in the United States. They once roamed across a very large part of the southwest, threatening more sedentary tribes like the Pueblo Indians of New Mexico and the Hopi of Arizona. Today, Navajo Indians are confined to a sprawling reservation that covers northern Arizona and northwestern New Mexico, southern Utah, and extreme southwestern Colorado. All Navajo territory is semi-arid desert land which is suitable habitat for the coyote.

Many Navajo eke out a scanty existence by herding large flocks of sheep, the only cash crop that can be raised on their desolate land. Coyotes have killed an alarming percentage of the sheep flock of individual herders, bringing great economic loss to the often impoverished Navajo.

Despite this destructive quality, the coyote is semi-revered in Navajoland. His resourcefulness and endurance are admired by an

Indian people who are noted for the same qualities. The Navajo may see the coyote as a parallel to their own existence—for both coyote and Navajo fight to stay alive in a red rock country where the rain seldom falls and very little grows; where strong hot winds parch the landscape seven months of the year and cold winds blow drifting snow for another four.

In the early 1960s many Navajos petitioned their leaders to do something to reduce the numbers of coyotes preying on the precious sheep. From the tribal council the request went to the deliberative session at Window Rock, Arizona; then on to the "Great White Father"—the federal government represented by the much-maligned Bureau of Indian Affairs. (Some Navajos at that time claimed that the initials BIA stood for "bastards in authority".) From BIA the request for assistance was passed on to its sister agency, Fish and Wildlife Service.

It was clear the reservation was home to entirely too many coyotes if you wanted to raise sheep. Buzz Fawcett, a paleface stationed on the Navajo reservation by the Fish and Wildlife Service, was one of the few white men who seemed to enjoy the full confidence of the Navajo. He had earned that trust by working closely with the Indians for years. He thoroughly understood and adapted to the Indian customs.

Buzz Fawcett allowed me to ride along to look over the situation. As we rode over the starkly beautiful red rock "lunarscape," Buzz told me about the taboos of the Navajos—all of which he respected and strictly observed. He showed me a *hogan,* the eight-sided home built of logs and railroad ties, where a Navajo had recently passed away. According to Navajo tradition, it was *chin-dee* (forbidden) to pass through the yard of the house where death had claimed a victim. To warn any passerby, the family of the dead person had pulled one log out of the wall, so that it stood at right angles to the wall. We could have saved ourselves five miles of driving on poor roads by simply driving through the yard with the death house, but Buzz wouldn't do it.

I don't believe he believed in the *chin-dee,* but Buzz honored the Navajo taboo. "If I drive this car through that yard, somebody will know it, and the Navajos will think I've gone crazy," he explained, "It's better to drive around and stay in good with the people I live with."

When Buzz Fawcett presented his evidence, the Fish and Wildlife Service agreed that there was a tremendous overpopulation of coyotes (by any standard) on the reservation and recommended a program of "chemical control;" a euphemism for poisoning by means of Compound 1080, *sodium monofluoracetate,* the highly selective predacide which was so deadly to canines and felines.

The Navajos discussed whether or not to poison their little brother at an indeterminable length over many council fires from Ganado to Tuba City and Teec Nos Pos to Burnt Water. Several years went by, along with those years' lambing seasons when the coyotes took a fearful toll of newborn lambs in many flocks. Hearing nothing from the Navajos, the Fish and Wildlife Service asked Buzz Fawcett to sound out his Navajo friends and report on the wishes of the Indians.

Buzz reported that the informal voting had been almost equally split, but the general consensus was that the poisoning should not take place. "But that could change at any minute," Buzz added.

Before the next lambing season rolled around, the word went out over the Indian telegraph that there would be a meeting at one of the Chapter Houses. They would "hold a dance" to decide the coyote question. Navajos traveled as far as one hundred miles to come to the meeting. Some arrived two or three days ahead of the meeting date, and stayed with the Navajo clan living there at the Chapter House. They expected to be fed by their hosts, even as they would have fed the Navajo strangers who came to their fires. They all were fed, though the residents sacrificed a great deal.

On the day of the "dance" the tom-toms beat far into the night. Speaker after speaker got up to address the throng, each of them relating some bit of wisdom about coyotes and sheep from the past. One speaker reminded the audience that the coyote was their little brother. Another speaker said that the coyote had lived harmoniously with the Navajo long before the white man's sheep were introduced. He suggested that they all get rid of the sheep. He obviously did not own any sheep.

A college-educated Navajo made a pragmatic, practical speech. "We try to feed our families," he said, "and the sheep is the best bet on these desert lands onto which the paleface has forced us to live. It is true that the coyote is my little brother, but if my little brother eats too much mutton, my children do not eat at all. If we share our food with the coyote, he becomes more numerous and our children grow weak with hunger."

Finally, everyone slept; you could assume that the meeting was adjourned. Actually, it was impossible to adjourn. No one person would claim to having enough authority to call a halt. If any decision had been reached, it was not apparent to paleface eyes.

49

When the winter sun was again high in the blue Arizona sky, the people began to troop into the meeting hall again. A group of elders gathered several hundred yards to the west of the Chapter House and built a small ceremonial fire. They hunkered down beside the fire and took turns sprinkling the fire with tiny bits of pollen and weed seeds they had carried in leather medicine pouches hidden in the folds of their clothing.

Beside the tiny fire, whose smoke rose straight up in the still air, the elders chanted. The meanings were lost in the mists of antiquity, but the effectiveness was recognized from the oral traditions of the people. The prayer song completed, each man pressed a stick into the softened ground, arranging them so that the upper ends of the sticks met to form a rude tripod over the fire. Then they stood erect and faced the Sacred Mountain far to the west and chanted the words again, at the same time kicking dirt over the fire to kill it. Then they turned to walk into the Chapter House and continue the meeting.

When they were nearly to the Chapter House, they saw young Navajos pointing to the fire which they had just extinguished. A crow had flown down and landed on top of the stick tripod. They all watched as the bird flopped down to the ground and searched for bits of food that it expected to be left beside a cooking fire. Finding none, the crow flew away.

Word came that the Navajos had decided against the use of 1080 once again. When I asked why, I was given the truthful answer, "Because a crow landed on top of the fire."

One year later, without any preliminaries, the Navajos asked for a coyote poisoning program. Compound 1080 was used and the coyote population was reduced by about 90 percent. The balance restored, Navajos again were in harmony with their little brother.

Chapter 10

Losing the War against Coyotes

Many people feel that the Vietnamese mistake was the first war that the United States didn't win. That isn't true. For forty-five years, Uncle Sam has fought a war against coyotes . . . and lost! In the years between 1937 and 1981, minions of the Fish and Wildlife Service scalped 3,612,220 coyotes. The ears with a connecting strip of skin were sent to a central tallying point as proof of their "body count." In 1982 there were probably more coyotes in the United States than ever before. Don't tell me that we didn't lose that war.

Let me repeat the total of coyotes killed from 1937 through 1981, so that the enormity of the casualty list sinks in. It was 3,612,220 verified coyotes deaths!

How accurate was that count? When coyotes are taken in traps, the count is absolutely correct. The only time a trapper may lose a scalp is when another predator eats the trapped animal, or if a fur trapper steals the animal from the trap. This loss, statistically, is negligible. When coyotes are killed with cyanide loaded coyote-getters, the loss probably runs about 10 percent. I estimate that cyanide kills in less than two minutes; yet, in that two minutes the coyote can put a lot of distance between his dying body and the getter location. Traps set in tall grass, or heavy brush country, will lose some. Some trappers will search for hours to find the kill, others take a quick look around and, not seeing the coyote, reset the device and go on about their work.

With strychnine poisoning, there was considerable loss. When Compound 1080 was in use from about 1945 through 1971, the losses went way, way up. 1080 was not a swift killer; the doomed animals would travel as much as a mile from the bait station before dying. It is my personal opinion that when 1080 was used, less than half of the dead coyotes were ever officially tallied. I would estimate that an additional three million coyotes were killed during that time but not tallied.

If my calculations are reasonable, coyotes suffered six million casualties in this war with Uncle Sam. Yet, we would have to admit that the coyotes have won the war.

Only one weapon was truly effective against coyotes—Compound 1080. When President Nixon banned its use on public lands, the coyote population immediately grew. There were probably more coyotes in the United States in 1982 than at any time in the known history of our nation.

Today the coyote is found in every continental state of the union. The traditional home range—Texas, New Mexico, Oklahoma, Colorado, Utah, and Wyoming—certainly now has a higher population of *Canis latrans* than at any point in my lifetime.

The year by year tabulation of "scalped" coyotes from 1937 through 1981 is shown below:

1937	80,299	1952	50,661	1967	75,892
1938	84,844	1953	55,000	1968	69,408
1939	93,039	1954	52,636	1969	73,956
1940	104,072	1955	55,204	1970	76,735
1941	110,495	1956	55,402	1971	75,661
1942	111,076	1957	62,585	1972	71,300
1943	103,971	1958	62,765	1973	76,454
1944	108,050	1959	78,714	1974	71,777
1945	102,979	1960	94,769	1975	81,910
1946	108,311	1961	100,363	1976	84,499
1947	103,982	1962	104,787	1977	68,218
1948	90,270	1963	89,653	1978	60,983
1949	75,448	1964	97,096	1979	65,341
1950	66,281	1965	90,236	1980	54,476
1951	60,455	1966	77,258	1981	57,178

The unequal war between federal government and coyotes really began in 1914, when Texas congressmen—pushed hard by sheep interests—wangled an appropriation bill through congress

to kill coyotes. Leadership of the coyote control operation in Texas was then in the hands of a young Canadian-born man named Cedric R. Landon. For forty years C. R. Landon ran an exemplary operation in the Lone Star State, earning the respect of friend and foe for his honest and straightforward dealings with the program's supporters. At the same time, Texas livestock interests began voluntarily taxing themselves to support a larger program than the federal government would have financed. This financial cooperation has continued to the present day, certainly indicating that those most vitally concerned felt that the program was economically necessary. Texas banks at times made it a condition to the granting of a "livestock-secured" loan that the livestock operator be a financial contributor to the cooperative program of coyote control.

We will take a further look at the special situation in Texas in the next chapter.

In the battle to reduce coyote numbers, the various federal Fish and Wildlife agencies (called the Bureau of Biological Survey, the Bureau of Sport Fisheries and Wildlife, and the Fish and Wildlife Service at various times) used many weapons. Among these were poisons such as strychnine and thallium sulfate, leghold traps, *Humane coyote-getters* ™ (discussed at length in Chapter 16) snares, den-hunting with destruction of the young coyotes, aerial hunting from planes, and—by far the most effective, Compound 1080, the subject of Chapter 18.

The historical background of the Federal government's attempts to stop coyote depredations follows many courses.

The following material is condensed from a report of the (then) Bureau of Biological Survey, written in 1939:

In the United States, the history of attempts to effect some degree of predator control, mainly through the bounty plan, may be divided into (1) the Colonial period (1630 to 1775) when practically every colony had some form of bounty plan in effect, (2) the period (1776 to 1865) of our territorial growth and developing statehood, to the close of the Civil War, when the new territories and States continued the expansion of the bounty plan, the older States increasing their efforts by legislating larger bounty payments, and (3) the period (1866 to 1939) of heaviest mortality from predator depredations, due to the growth of the profitable livestock industry in the West. This period saw the rise of the bounty plan to its peak, and the gradual reduction of it by substituting the present coordinated plan of cooperation with the Federal Government.

The first attempts at wolf control via the bounty method were through action taken by the early law makers of Massachusetts in 1630, followed by that of the Grand Assembly at Jamestown, Colonial Virginia, on September 4, 1632. The wolf had become an outlaw in the minds of those early settlers, because of its ruthless depredations against sheep and cattle. From the comments of Clayton and other early colonial authorities it appears that wolves had held back the development of the sheep industry in Virginia for the better part of the seventeenth century.

. . . . following a bounty system similar to that adopted in other colonies, Pennsylvania, under the governorship of William Penn, developed the unique system of employing what probably was the first professional wolf hunter in North America to be financed by a commonwealth. The act was passed in 1705 . . . . (remember that these wolves in the original colonies and the original 13 states were really wolves and not coyotes) . . . .

In 1790, David Thompson, the pioneer geographer of the far West, referring to the western plains, commented, "They are well adapted for raising cattle and when the wolves are destroyed, also for sheep." (he referred to both wolves and coyotes here in the west.) . . . . In the early part of 1843, the citizens of Willamette Valley, Oregon, called a meeting known in Oregon history as the "wolf meeting" for the purpose of formulating . . . . measures for protection against predatory animals. Thus the very first meeting of the settlers in Oregon had to do with the problems of predators . . . . part of the nineteenth century wolf control was a common subject of discussion among those participating in the cattle roundups on the plains. Among measures adopted was a range law whereby no rancher riding the range would knowingly pass up a dead carcass without inserting in it a goodly dose of strychnine, in the hope of eventually killing a wolf or two. The hazard to other forms of wildlife of such use of strychnine was not apparent to the stock interests at the time.

I have found that almost every account of the early days of coyote-vs-man in the west includes reference to the range custom of every cowboy carrying a vial of strychnine to "lace" every carcass of a range animal that he chanced upon in his day's riding.

John C. Gatlin, who completed nearly fifty years of work with the Bureau of Sport Fisheries and Wildlife, most of that attached to the Branch of Predator and Rodent Control, gave me an interesting sidelight on this bit of folklore.

"Chuck, I've heard that business of cowboys sticking strychnine into every carcass they found on the plains. I've heard it all my life. But I never knew a cowboy who ever carried strychnine for this purpose. Nor did I ever hear of any during the years I was supervising coyote control over an eight state area in the middle of the coyotes—and wolf's—range. Like so many stories about the Old West, it is so plumb logical that it's a shame that it isn't true."

I place a lot of faith in John Gatlin's knowledge of pioneer cowboy days. His career started with Uncle Sam trying to catch Pancho Villa in 1917, and lasted through all of the intensive coyote control work of the Fish and Wildlife Service up to 1967.

The 1939 Report continues:

Practically all of the Western states and many of the counties had tried bounties for years, following the example set by the older states in the East, some with disastrous results, and it was felt that this plan was far from adequate. Field naturalists of the Survey made investigations of depredations upon livestock and wild game. These led to published reports by the Department of Agriculture, as "Coyotes in their Economic Relations" (1905), "Directions for the Destruction of Wolves and Coyotes" (1907) and "Key to Animals on which Wolf and Coyote Bounties are often Paid" (1909).

In 1914, as a result of the continuous pressure from the West for further governmental assistance against the menace that the bounty had not been able to combat, the Congress made a small appropriation for experiments and demonstrations in predatory animal control mainly to find out what could be done. In 1915 the first sizable appropriation was made, $125,000, and the language of the act called for direct participation by the Biological Survey in control work instead of mere instruction. It directly ordered the destruction of wolves, coyotes, and other animals injurious to agriculture and animal husbandry on the national forests and the public domain, and thus definitely took out of the hands of the Forest Service the fight it had been waging since 1905, making it a part of the regular work of the (Biological) Survey.

An outbreak of rabies in the Oregon country, and elsewhere, brought appropriations totalling $200,000 for the control of rabid animals, using the predatory animal control forces already formed. The entire West was included with eight districts being set up to administer the work. Slightly less than 16,000 animals were destroyed during that year.

The coyote . . . . readily adapts itself and thrives under conditions incident to livestock and agricultural expansion. These remarkable qualities of the coyote have been responsible for the great extension of its range. Formerly this included the western plains and basal mountain slopes from western Canada and the United States south over the tableland of Mexico and the tropical savannas along the Pacific Coast as far south as Costa Rica, but in recent years the range has been extended northward from British Columbia into the Yukon Territory and thence into the Yukon Valley and has reached Point Barrow, Alaska and the mouth of the Mackenzie River in Canada. This extension of range has also been westward to the Northwest Coast, eastward into the North Central States, and more recently to Maine, New York, Pennsylvania, Virginia, New Jersey, South Carolina, Georgia, Florida, Mississippi, and Tennessee. . . . Because of the coyote's ability to adapt itself to changing environment concern need not be felt over the possibility of its ever becoming extinct or even approaching extinction in North America. . . .

It is very difficult to arrive at a definite figure representing the aggregate monetary losses occasioned by the depredations of predators and rodents, though one can state with a reliable degree of assurance that the total losses sustained in the United States annually run into a considerable sum of money. The enormity of big game losses due to predators is evidenced by reports of the Forest Service, which indicate that during the year 1936, predators destroyed 129,152 big game animals on national forests alone . . . . the same year the Forest Service reported 78,404 sheep and goats killed by predators on the national forests. . . .

Coyotes and wolves are inflicting severe losses on Alaskan reindeer through direct killings and dispersal of herds, as is typified by a report from a reindeer company near Skugnak . . . . (*this loss seems to be attributable to wolves, not coyotes: Author*)

Prior to 1937, the largest sheep-raising outfit in Nevada reported annual losses of 8 to 10 percent of its herds through coyote depredation, and these losses continued until a Biologi-

57

cal Survey hunter was assigned to the area in the fall of 1937.

A rancher in Montrose County, Colorado, recently lost forty lambs during a two week period because of a crippled coyote; and a rancher in northwestern Colorado lost sixty head of sheep within twenty days through coyote depredations. During the past year, an Arizona rancher lost 15 percent of his sheep during a drive of twenty-five miles, and a ranching company at Battle Mountain, Nevada, reported losses of 25 to 35 percent of the lamb crop from a band of five thousand sheep, all as a result of coyote depredation.

The increase in the number of coyotes *(1939, remember)* is reflected in the steady upward curve of predator catch from year to year as compiled from reports of the Biological Survey's hunters, the number of predatory animals taken by those hunters in 1938 being approximately 100 percent greater than that for the year 1931, although the funds available for work during 1938 were only 15 percent greater than in 1931. Partial explanation can be found in the matter of increased efficiency of the Bureau's hunters, but the main reason for such an increased take in 1938 is better ascribed to the greater number of coyotes at large.

The remainder of this 1939 report consists of a discussion of the pros and cons of having a professional group of coyote trappers, the extent to which financial support of the predator control program is bolstered by cooperating agencies and individuals, and the fact that livestock interests are willing to tax themselves to help defray the costs of the Bureau of Biological Survey's coyote control program. The entire report is recommended reading for the serious student of coyote control systems.

The earliest employees of the predator control division of the Bureau of Biological Survey were the field men—the trappers or hunters. What kind of men were they?

Chapter 11

The Government Trapper

Since the federal government initiated its campaign against the coyote way back in 1914, thousands of men have been employed as field workers. They are known as government trappers, federal hunters—or simply "the federal coyote man." Near the Mexican border they were often known as "El Coyotero."

There was a tremendous diversity in this ever-changing field force. Hired from different walks of life, to face different challenges in different environments, the coyote men had only a few things in common. There was little commonality between the coyote trapper named Agapito Flores, down near the Rio Grande in Texas, and Bob Wahlin at Ipswich, South Dakota. Agapito spoke Spanish better than he spoke English; Bob, a former school teacher, spoke only English. Bob followed his pack of hounds across the icy winter fields of South Dakota. Agapito used coyote-getters almost 100 percent of the time and killed coyotes where it seldom stays cold more than an hour or two.

Federal hunter Cecil Albers of Spearfish, South Dakota, was a specialist who successfully shot coyotes with an autoloading shotgun from the seat of a light airplane on the flat prairies of his state. He was good at his job.

Odie Roberts was a lion hunter in the Big Bend of Texas. A good horseman, hound dog man and mule trainer, Roberts spent all of his time chasing after mountain lions. He was good at his job, too.

Carl Baker, trapper supervisor in the Texas Panhandle, prepares a meal for his den hunting partners.

There was one common denominator among the federal trappers. They were the best outdoorsmen I have ever known. They were more in tune with the natural environment than any group of game wardens, biologists, federal game management agents, forest rangers, or other group of outdoor workers I'd ever met. Not all of them, of course, but those who lacked this finely-tuned sensitivity to what went on around them didn't last long. There was a second common denominator, they were universally poorly paid. Obviously, the man who made a good trapper wasn't in it for the bucks. If a man was more interested in money than trapping, he soon left. If he wasn't a good outdoorsman, it quickly showed in his lack of results, and he was replaced.

The ability to read sign is a requisite of all good outdoorsmen, and many federal hunters were skilled beyond any telling of it. I've had the pleasure of working with a few of them, and learning from many of them.

In western South Dakota, Walden Lemm was the airplane pilot for the Branch of Predator and Rodent Control. His headquarters were in Spearfish where the plane was kept. The purchase of the plane was an example of the special relationship which existed between ranchers and the coyote hunters who served them. The plane was purchased by the South Dakota Woolgrowers, who collected the money by passing the hat at their annual meeting. Nobody dropped greenbacks or silver into the hat; the usual donation was a good-sized check, for airplanes did not come cheaply—even in the 1950s.

The plane was registered in the name of the Woolgrowers. The cost of licensing, insuring, and maintenance was borne by the U.S. Fish and Wildlife Service through the terms of an impromptu agreement. When Walden Lemm thought that the plane was getting a little long in the tooth, he told the Woolgrowers so. They told him to go ahead and make a trade-in deal. He did, and the Woolgrowers made up the "to-boot" money by passing the hat again.

I can still remember the look on the face of the federal government auditor when he spotted this informal agreement. "You can't spend federal funds to insure a privately owned plane," he said, "and you can't order federal employees to fly in a plane owned by the Woolgrowers."

The Woolgrowers felt that a handshake was every bit as good as a federal contract. They thought we could continue the way we had been doing. The informal agreement continued to work for many years.

Walden piloted the plane and shotgunners picked off the running coyotes as he brought them down close into point blank range. Cecil Albers did a lot of the shooting; so did Ralph Block. There were others. I did a little of it, but never could claim that I was proficient at it. The feeling that you are going to get airsick at any moment is an inhibiting factor. Several times I was right, too.

It was the tracking ability of Walden Lemm that I remember. He could sort out the patterns of black holes in the snow from the air, which marked where a coyote had traveled. Keeping the location of one set of tracks in his mind as he found another, he could zero-in on a den full of pups by watching the pattern of tracks in the rotting snows of early spring. A feeding or hunting coyote meanders along; the adult returning to disgorge food for the pups goes pretty much on a beeline course.

We were hunting for a particularly damaging pair of coyotes in the Edgemont area south of the Black Hills, using two crews of two men each in four wheel drive pickups, and the airplane. Activities were coordinated by using war surplus two-way radios. The ground crews had parked their vehicles and were combing the area on foot. Walden soared above, studying the scant evidence in the fast-disappearing snows. After ten minutes of looking at this one section area, Walden called me on the radio, "Chuck, there's what looks like a den right at the base of that straight up and down clay bank to the south of you about two hundred yards. I bet that's where she got her pups."

I walked over and checked the hole he had found. There was only dry, dusty dirt at the entrance, and for fifty feet in every direction in front of it. I searched the area but found no sign of coyote. I knelt with my ear at the mouth of the burrow, listening intently for the sounds of pups at play. Nothing. Knowing that tracks would be hard to find in the hardbaked soil in front of the den, I circled around, looking for tracks in the patches of snow. Nothing!

My walkie-talkie cracked, "What do you think, Chuck?"

"That's not it, Walden," I came back, "no sign at all down here."

The plane lifted a wingtip and went sliding off to the south, starting the search anew. But ten more minutes of flying south, east and north of that cutbank den brought Walden to the same conclusion. It just had to be that den. He swung low to study the dirt road to the west of our position, then turned into the wind and did a "zero roll" landing on that section line road. Getting out, Walden walked to one of the trucks and took out a shovel. As I watched in amazement, he went straight to the cutbank den and gave the arm wave signal that meant, "Come and get 'em; this is it!"

When I joined him at the den site, Walden looked at me sorrowfully and said, "Chuck, it sure is hard to get good help these days!" In the entry to the den there were three round wet spots, and in each wet spot there were the unmistakeable tracks of coyote pups! After an hour of hard digging, we were able to cable out seven pups by using a piece of telephone guy-wire with the ends unraveled and bent back to form hooks. An expert with this tool could tangle it in the hide of any coyote and pull him, protesting, to his fate.

No amount of protesting on my part would convince Walden that those telltale pup prints were not there when I looked.

This man could read the sign from the air better than I had on the ground, and was confident enough of his own diagnosis to land his plane and come over to prove it. I salute him—expert tracker, careful and skilled pilot, and one of the best rifle shots I've ever seen.

Speaking of rifle shots—Texas subdistrict supervisor E. G. Pope won the thousand yard shoot with iron sights when he was 65 years old. Tracking problems were different in Texas, where rocky ground and gravel so often make it hard to find evidence. Mr. Pope had two "straw bosses" named Carl Baker and Tom Sparks, and the three of them made a wonderfully skilled tracking triumvirate.

Because the bosses emphasized tracking ability, so did the field men. The spring of the year always featured my trip to the Lubbock Subdistrict for two weeks of den hunting. I used to look forward to that two weeks with fear and anticipation. Fear because my desk-softened body took a fearful beating during the twelve hour days these men put in walking or shoveling. Anticipation, because I learned more about tracking from these experts than any other source.

Working with a trapper named Childress, in Childress County, Pope, Baker, Sparks, and I sought a killer coyote that had already taken a heavy toll from a nearby lambing flock. Señor coyote resided in a six-square-mile tract of red sand and gullies near the Red River. We went to the hunt area in two vehicles, then spread out to walk the maze of sagebrush, creosote bush, and gullies. We headed in the general direction of the Red River.

Fifteen minutes into the hunt, I saw Carl Baker waving his arm from atop a nob of dirt pointing in a straight line to the northward. A few minutes later Tom was making a similar signal from far to the west. The line of position he indicated would bisect the one Carl had given us, about two miles north of my position. I angled more sharply northward trying to locate a coyote track. I found nothing. Then a shrill whistle from Mr. Childress gave another straight line signal, to bisect the other two lines of position just a few hundred yards north of my position. I picked up the pace, searching intently for another track. I found nothing. All four of my *compañeros* were converging on me.

I waited for them and was embarrassed to find that I was waiting within twenty feet of the very active den located at the base of a big brushy pile. No one alluded to the fact that I had walked over, through, around, and past a dozen lines of tracks whose discovery would have brought us to the den sooner. Usually, we dug out the dens so that we could scalp the pups and add them to the total. If it was difficult or dangerous to dig them out, we tossed a couple of smoke cylinders down the den, closed the entrance with a couple of shovels of dirt and went on about our business.

Carl Baker told me once that he doubted that I could track a bulldozer through his grandson's sandbox, but I really wasn't that bad. I learned, after a while, not to look for tracks, but rather to look for the single toenail scratch left by a running coyote, for the bit of disturbed soil, the tiny flake of rock turned up on edge, even the bent grass on a dewy morning. Either Baker, Sparks or Pope could follow a trail at a fast walk—a trail which I couldn't find after they told me it was there. Nothing wrong with my eyesight, I just hadn't developed that ability to interpret what I did see, to get the complete story from a tiny scratch on a smooth rock.

E. G. Pope was somewhat of a martinet and disciplinarian who worked his field force as hard as he worked himself. As Carl Baker once told me in a moment of candor, "That man is sometimes hard to get along with, but I guess I wouldn't take for him." In case you aren't familiar with the language of Texas, that means that he wouldn't want to trade Mr. Pope for another supervisor.

Digging out coyote dens can get a bit hairy, especially in the sandy soils of west and north Texas. Tom and Carl did most of the shovel work on one den in Dallam County. The den angled sharply down twelve feet, and required a lot of earth moving. At the bottom, the den turned up and to the right. The den had probably been the work of an over-achiever badger which had been converted by the coyote mother for her own purposes. Tom slid head first down our long excavation to look around the curve with a flashlight, and to listen. He came scuttling backwards out of the hole, "I don't think there's anything in there," he said glumly.

"Tracks say she's using this den," Pope opined, and he took the flashlight to take a look himself. Now, during the time between when Tom came up and Pope went down, something very much alive moved down in that den. E. G. Pope slid head first down the sloping tunnel, stuck his head around the corner and gave a startled yelp. With amazing speed, he came flying backward, feet first, up out of the tunnel! He had found himself staring a diamondback rattler in the face from a distance of six inches when he peered around the corner. Tom went back down, did some spade work which cut off the rattlesnake's head, then widened the tunnel at the entrance. We worked the cable back into the den and "wired out" one female coyote and six pups.

Snakes weren't the only creatures we found living with a den full of coyotes. Porcupines sought shelter in these big dens in areas where trees were scarce. Once we slid a cable past a coyote and hooked it into a porky. When we slowly brought the porky out, the coyote came on out ahead of him—choosing the un-known danger above over the known danger of painful quills from the very irate porcupine.

Even Carl Baker didn't see everything, however. When he was concentrating on following a coyote track, he overlooked every-thing else but the track. Working with a government trapper named Malcolm O'Bannon, Carl and I helped search a huge sandy area, but found no tracks. We all headed for the pickup truck, about a mile away. Nearing the truck, Carl found himself ahead of Malcolm and me, so he stopped, leaning on his longhandled shovel, to wait for us. I came up and joined him, and we waited for Malcolm.

Malcolm was a slow-talking Texan. He came up close to us, leaned on his shovel and then slowly drawled, "Carl . . . big as Texas is . . . you'd think you could find someplace else to stand . . . 'cept near that rattlesnake." Carl looked down; then jumped four feet straight up. He had been standing within inches of a coiled up sidewinder rattlesnake. As he expertly spaded off the snake's head, he said, "I purely hate to kill this snake. It acted like a gentleman."

The expert outdoorsman is above all, a good observer. But in addition to seeing what goes on out-of-doors, he must also have a lot of common sense, and an ability to recognize what is possible and what is not. Dean Badger was a federal trapper in South Dakota, a soft-spoken man who had stored up a world of lore in a lifetime in the outdoors. He used steel traps to try to take a very wily, sheep-killing coyote that was preying upon a small farm flock just west of Gettysburg, South Dakota. I joined him on his first visit to the farm to see what the complaint was. We walked all over the pasture, and finally found the tracks of the coyote where he came through a narrow, rain-carved gully from the creek bed up to the grassland. Very carefully, Dean set a *#3 Newhouse* trap there, covering the trap pan with an old piece of light canvas which had wintered in the dry sheep manure. Then he carefully sprinkled a thin film of dust over the trap cloth and the jaws of the trap. Using a turkey tail feather—flight featers are too stiff—he added the final touches to his artistry. There was no visible sign of the trap or of the chain.

The next day, after completion of his other duties, we went out to check the single trap. It was not sprung, but the track of the coyote showed plainly. He had actually stepped on the trap cloth over the jaw, not over the pan. By an eighth of an inch, the coyote had missed springing the trap. Dean carefully used his turkey feather to smooth out the sign, leaving the trap as before, a masterpiece of concealment. The next day, the same thing happened. By an eighth of an inch the coyote had again missed the trigger pan, while actually stepping on the trap. His footprint was in exactly the same position as it had been the day before.

Noting that Dean was going to smooth it over again, not change it, I offered a suggestion, "Dean, maybe we ought to move that trap a half an inch so that the pan will be where he has been stepping."

Dean looked at me with disgust, "Chuck, I can make the coyote step on my trap, but only God can make him step on the pan." The third day the coyote was caught.

Knowing where to set the trap is 90 percent of the battle when using leghold traps. The Texas District, Predator and Rodent Control had an urgent call from rancher Steve Stumberg, saying that a lion had killed a valuable quarter horse colt, one with just the right markings that Steve had been breeding toward. He was upset and angry, and wanted that lion taken right now. Our Number One lion man was Odie Roberts, but Odie was on another assignment in the far reaches of Brewster County and couldn't be reached. We asked government trapper Earl Baker, a giant of a man, to take his big traps over to Stumberg's ranch and see what he could do. Earl protested that he wasn't a lion trapper and that he only had three big traps, but agreed to do what he could. When he got to the ranch, one of the hands drove him to the top of the rimrock and showed him where the lion had made the kill. Earl carried his traps and trap-setting gear along.

Starting near the kill, Earl circled out in ever-sidening loops, searching for signs of the cat's travel lanes. A quarter of a mile from the kill, he found the track of a big tom in six inches of soft sand between big boulders. The cat had—one time, at least—used that pathway to gain access to the horse pasture. Carefully, Earl set a trap there, then went on looking for more places to set. It got dark and he still hadn't found a good place to set another trap. A good trapper knows that it doesn't make sense to set a trap just anywhere. So Earl hung the other big traps on the barbed wire fence and headed home.

When he returned the next morning, a jubilant Stumberg met him with the words, "You got that damned lion, a big tom. My man killed him with a rope this morning!" After accepting a congratulatory handshake, Earl allowed as how he had to go up and skin the lion, and recover his traps. The pelts were being donated to wildlife management classes at that time.

The happy Mr. Stumberg offered to drive him up on the rimrock. After Earl separated the lion from his pelt, and stowed that one trap in the back of the jeep, Stumberg asked, "Where's the rest of your traps?" Earl pointed down the fence line and they drove that way. When Earl picked the two traps off the fence and said, "That's it," Stumberg asked, "You mean to tell me that you only set one trap?"

Earl's answer earned him a place in my pantheon of memorable trappers. He said, "There wasn't but one lion!"

We could talk on about a hundred more government trappers, but we will meet more of them in the chapters about their control methods. The tools of the government coyote trapper were the steel leghold trap, the coyote-getter, strychnine poison, thallium sulphate poison, Compound 1080, den hunting, calling the coyote to within gun range, and aerial hunting—first from fixed wing aircraft and then from helicopters.

The government trappers formed a motley crew, as varied as it is possible to be—but all were good outdoorsmen who considered the coyote a worthy adversary.

Chapter 12

The Special Case of Texas

A large part of Texas was included in the range of the coyote before Columbus brought the blight of European invasion to these shores. With the exception of the forested eastern portion where the red wolf (probably) held sway, all of Texas was well suited to coyote living.

For many years, Texas was the biggest sheep and goat producer in the nation. In Texas, the coyote has been fought—longer, harder, and stronger—than in any other state. The government program for the control of predatory animals got its start, in terms of actual "coyote-killing" operation in Texas. The coyote control program employed far more men, had more public support, and was pressed more strenuously in Texas than in any other state.

But in the early 1980s there are more coyotes in Texas than in any other state.

In coyote control, as in many other things, the Sovereign Empire of Texas has a law unto itself. Things really are different in Texas.

On January 30, 1909, approximately one hundred sheep and goat raisers met in San Angelo, Texas, and organized the Wool Growers Control Storage Company. The meeting was described by an eloquent writer for the local paper, in the typical over-blown rhetoric of the day, as being "A Notable Assembly of Wit,

Wisdom and Wealth—Conclave of Veteran Flock Masters." The newspaper article of February 6, 1909, went on to say, "Make way for the men who own the flocks that clothe the world and which roam the hills and browse in the sunny vales from the Rio Grande to the cottonfields of the Colorado—from the Panhandle to Padre Island—was the slogan in San Angelo Saturday."

The sheepmen gathered to form a cooperative to market their wool, to secure credit at easier terms than they were used to paying, and to try to reduce their losses to wolf and coyote predation. The predation problem was approached with a resolution which called on the state of Texas to pay a bounty for the scalps of wolves and coyotes. The reasoning behind this plea is best explained by looking at the situation which prevailed in the rough and rugged lands of west Texas, where the greatest numbers of sheep and goats were run.

Using Mexican sheepherders—because they were available at very low wages—these sheep raisers herded their flocks by day and brought them into pens for closer protection at night. It was customary to set lanterns around the pens, for the predators were numerous and very bold. Any sheep or goats left out on the main pasture at nightfall probably would not live to see the light of day. Sheep men customarily budgeted a loss of at least one tenth of their herd each year, due to predation.

Knowing that a large group of his constituents were solidly behind the fight against coyotes, State Senator Hudspeth, with the assistance of Mr. Brown F. Lee, got the state legislature to pass a bounty law in 1911. The state appropriated $100,000, to be disbursed at the rate of five bucks per wolf and one dollar per coyote scalp brought in for payment. Because county clerks could not differentiate, some counties called all of the scalps timber wolves, others were calling every scalp a coyote. Because of this problem, the state legislators decided to bring the payments nearer to parity to eliminate overpayment when they passed another appropriation for bounty payments in 1915. The wolf fee was set at two dollars and the coyote at one dollar. Remember that a dollar bought a lot more in 1915 than it does today.

In 1912, sheepman Sam H. Hill built a woven wire fence around his sheep flock, eliminating the need for Mexican herders. The success of this first "coyote-proof" fence brought on imitators, and early reports show that the sheepmen of west Texas competed with each other to build the most protective fence. At the same time, many of these men employed packs of hounds for the purpose of running down and killing any coyote that succeeded in finding his way into the "coyote-proof" exclosure.

Bounty payments have never reduced the numbers of any predator anywhere in North America, and this one didn't do much to help the sheepmen of west Texas, either. Despite the hounds, despite the improved availability of steel traps, and despite the bounty payments, the coyote still exacted a fearful toll of Texas sheep and goats.

Cedric R. Landon, who headed the government's predator control program in Texas for more years than any other man, summarized what happened next in Texas, when he wrote:

In the summer of 1914, some of the same men who had been present at the organization of the Wool Growers Control Storage Company three years earlier, through Sam H. Hill, solicited the assistance of the Federal government. The first government hunters were employed on a temporary basis in the fall of that year and the work was established on a permanent basis in July of 1915.

During the next four years, the sheep and goat raisers generally became convinced that the systematic, organized work of the government hunters was more effective in reducing losses from predators than the unsupervised work of the bounty trappers. The latter naturally elected to work where predators were numerous and were not too much interested in trying to catch the few in the proximity of the sheep pastures where most of the losses occurred.

In 1919, State Senator C. B. Hudspeth, with the help of Senator Julius Real and of M. E. Blackburn, the member of the House from Junction, succeeded in passing the first bill providing for cooperation between the State and Federal Governments in predator control. This bill carried an appropriation of $25,000 per year for two years and provided that no part of this should be expended on bounties.

When the next legislature convened in 1921, an unsuccessful attempt was made to secure State funds to continue this cooperation between the state and federal governments. When the state failed to contribute toward the cost of the program, the federal program was materially reduced and would have been withdrawn entirely if it had not been for the insistence of Claude Hudspeth who had left the State Senate to represent his district in Washington. From 1921 to 1927 an attempt was made each year to secure favorable action from the various legislatures which served during that period. The Sheep and Goat Raisers Association adopted resolutions in support of the work and its officers made several trips to Austin without success. The fox hunters associations, who are opposed to predator control because it interferes with their sport, were successful in blocking everything the stockmen tried to do during this period. The representatives from thinly populated west Texas were badly outnumbered by the men from the cities and thickly populated east Texas, who were either indifferent to the need for predator control or influenced by their fox hound owner constituents.

Finally, in 1927, the representative from Mason, Roscoe Runge, assisted by his good friend Jim Finley of Fife and others, after a hard fight, succeeded in securing passage of a bill providing $25,000 per year for predator control in the next two fiscal years. This resulted in a substantial increase in both federal and local cooperative funds available for the program. The year before the passage of this bill by the 40th legislature, only $27,000 was available from all sources. During the year after the passage of Mr. Runge's bill, this was increased to approximately $100,000.

To digress a bit, much attention should be paid to the name of Roscoe Runge, a very important prime mover in the world of Texas coyote control. When I met him in 1959, Judge Runge was no longer in the state legislature, but was still a respected voice in the discussions of the Texas Sheep and Goat Raisers Association, and of all the cooperative entities that helped pay the bill for coyote control in Texas. He was an expert at the "old school" type of oratory, with its hyperbole and its emotional appeals, which still is very effective in rural Texas. He was, and is, somewhat of a hero to many of the sheep growers of central and west Texas. The historical account of the beginnings of coyote control in Texas continues:

After the 41st legislature met in January 1929 it soon became apparent that the same uphill fight might be expected if the appropriation for predator control was to be continued or increased. The predator problem since 1920 has had to do principally with the control of coyotes and red or timber wolves. With lobos out of the picture, the losses caused the cattle industry by predators was comparatively slight. The Cattle Raisers Association has never taken more than a perfunctory interest in this control program. Many counties which were experiencing heavy losses of poultry, hogs, and small farm flocks of sheep and goats, were not organized with respect to predator control. With the very limited funds available from public appropriations, it was very difficult to extend this program into such counties. It was apparent that the support of the Texas Sheep and Goat Raisers Association alone was not sufficient to induce the state legislators to provide funds for a program which should be extended far beyond the area controlled by the members of that association.

In order to meet this situation, men who were vitally interested in the control of predators were invited to meet in Austin where the 41st legislature was in session. Over one hundred ranchmen, businessmen and farmers attended and on April 22, 1929, the Texas Predatory Animal Control Association was organized. The late Roy Hudspeth was elected President and John P. Classen, Secretary-Treasurer. It was decided to employ Roscoe Runge as attorney and legislative representative. Within a week, sufficient funds had been contributed by the members of the new association to take care of all expenses for the ensuing year.

Mr. Runge went to work at once and very skillfully crystallized the sentiment created by the delegation to Austin. Before the Austin meeting it had appeared very doubtful that any appropriation would be secured for the next biennium. As a result of the meeting and Mr. Runge's work, an appropriation of $70,000 per year was made. During the five years prior to the organization of the Texas Predatory Animal Control Association, the total funds available for predator control was $296,000 and 12,000 predators were taken. This was in the prosperous times in the late twenties when money was plentiful. During the five years after the Association was formed in 1929, during the worst of the depression years, a total of over $700,000 was made available and over 64,000 predators were taken. During the same time, the scope of the program was extended from twenty odd counties in west Texas to over one hundred counties over Texas generally. As a matter of fact at that time there were 42 counties in Texas with a very heavy predator infestation, 93 with a medium to light infestation, and 61 with a scattered or light infestation. In other words, predators constituted a problem in 196 out of the 254 Texas Counties.

The Texas Predatory Animal Control Association (TPACA) has been in operation ever since that organizational start in 1929. It has administered the funds of the Texas Cooperative Trapping Fund. The Trapping Fund got its funds through appropriation by the various County Commissioner's Courts and the so-called "Wolf Clubs"—many of which are still in existence.

A wolf club was an organization of sheep and goat raisers who voluntarily assessed themselves a certain amount of money, paid that money into the Trapping Fund and allowed the TPACA to disburse those funds to provide a government trapper work in their area. The TPACA has been such a great success for so many years for two reasons. One was the organizational genius of Judge Roscoe Runge; and the other—perhaps most important—is that the TPACA allows the ranchers to pay for their own protection. The TPACA collects its monies directly from the people who benefit most from the expenditure of those funds. It also operated at a very low overhead. For many years after its organization, Roscoe Runge was the only paid officer; the others served without pay. Even as late as 1959, when I began work in Texas, the TPACA had only one clerk on the payroll—no one else was paid.

Roy Hudspeth served as president of TPACA until his death, when he was replaced by Mark L. Browne, another of the giant figures that heroically strode across the path of the coyote—the type of bigger-than-life personage Texas seems to produce in quantity.

In earlier years Mark L. Browne had been entrusted with secrets while serving in China as a Marine. The white-haired, florid-complexioned Mark L. Browne had become a wealthy man; a director of several banks and the prime mover in the Texas Fat Stock Show in his home of San Antonio. An excellent speaker with an oratorical bent, Mark cut a commanding figure when he got up to talk. He had an air about him which commanded instant respect for his views. My favorite memory of him was in Big Spring, Texas, where he addressed the convention of the Texas Sheep and Goat Raisers Association. Bad news had just come from Austin, Texas, where the legislature was recalcitrant to appropriate monies for predator control. The legislature had just performed a slick act, but let's let Mark Browne tell it.

"I have just been informed, by sources I trust, that the legislature of the state of Texas, in its wisdom, has just transferred state supervision of the state's work in predator and rodent control from the efficient and friendly hands of the Texas A & M Extension Service, where it has been ably managed for these many years—to

74

the unfriendly hands of the State Game and Fish Department, which does not have either experience or expertise to handle the duty. In their lack of wisdom, the legislature has transferred this vital function to the Game and Fish Department, without an appropriation thereto. By this subterfuge, the legislature attempts to perform two actions—to cripple the vital functions of predator and rodent control, and to gain access to the sequestered funds of the Texas Game, Fish and Oyster Commission."

Mark paused a long moment for effect, his silver white hair flashing in the rays of the sun coming in through a side window, while he stared up to the ceiling as if seeking guidance from some higher authority. He must have found what he sought, for he continued—"In speaking of this action of the state legislature, the men we have voted into office and can vote out of office, one can only paraphrase the words of the Master, 'Father forgive them, for they know not what they do!!' "

The action of the legislative body, transferring the predator control work to the Game and Fish Department was later reversed, of course. State appropriated funds were funneled into the program through the Texas A & M University Extension Service, which closely supervised their part of the program. Other funds came from the TPACA, which had only very minimal supervision of their funds, as they customarily rubberstamped the decisions of the civil service federal employee who headed the entire program, and controlled the expenditures of federal funds. For many years the federal employee was Cedric R. Landon, the third "giant in the earth" in the saga of Texas Predator Control work. Mr. Landon was a transplanted Canadian in a state that usually has little time for "non-natives," yet he won the respect and friendship of not only the ranching community, but also the state legislative community. It was often remarked that "Mr. Landon won't lie to you; he simply wouldn't bother to give you any information that wasn't factual."

Financing the work of several hundred employees with funds from so many sources kept the office in San Antonio busy with some creative bookkeeping at times. Some government hunters got three different colored pay checks during the year; starting as federal employees, switching to state employees, and finally to TPACA employees as the funds were exhausted in these categories. An attempt was made to keep the best men on the federal payroll all year long, as this gave them a chance to accumulate a healthy federal retirement.

The main point in all this Texas history is that coyote control was begun to stop economic loss; it was paid for by ranchers who put their money where their mouths were; and it financed the most strenuous "all out" war against the coyote that the world has ever seen.

In 1959, the Texas program was under the supervision of Milton Caroline, a transplanted Connecticut Yankee who had earned his place as head of the program with a more than ten-year apprenticeship under C. R. Landon himself. There were six sub-district supervisors scattered through the Lone Star State. Darwin (Shorty) Ivy covered the trans-Pecos area and headed the office at Marva. Johnny White, a very tall Texan, supervised the north central part of Texas from his Fort Worth office. Calvin Johnson was the likeable administrator in the area of highest coyote density—south of Highway #90 including the coyote hatchery of Dimmit, Uvalde, Maverick, Zavala and Kinney counties. Hinton Bridgwater supervised the deepest south part of Texas from head-quarters in Edinburg. Jimmy Poore had a very small group of employees in the "red wolf" areas of south and east Texas, but was primarily the liaison with Texas A & M College with headquarters at College Station. The legendary E. G. Pope supervised the Panhandle of Texas. His Lubbock office usually had the greatest number of trappers on the payroll (it shifted from month to month).

Let's take a closer look at how this program was financed and administered. In Fiscal Year 1962, federal funds provided only 21 percent of the total Texas expenditures—yet provided all of the supervisors. Many Texas ranchers were quick to say that it was a case of the tail wagging the dog. The state of Texas furnished 41 percent of the funds, and the Texas Predatory Animal Control Association provided a total of 38 percent of the total. TPACA funds can be divided further to show that counties provided 25 percent of the total (more than the federal government did); individual associations (the "Wolf Clubs") provided 5 percent of the total funds; and most remarkable, individuals provided 8 percent of the total funds! It should be pointed out that there was no legal obligation on the part of the counties, TPACA associations, or TPACA individuals to renew their agreements from year to year. Every year those entities thought it over and voluntarily decided to continue to expend their money for the purpose of killing coyotes. Evidently, they felt they got their money's worth.

In 1962, the total of all funds available to the Texas District for all work was $948,307. Nearing one million dollars per year.

In 1962, there were 19 trappers in Shorty Ivy's subdistrict, 36 working under E. G. Pope, 37 under Johnny W. White, 29 under Calvin Johnson, 23 under Bob Shiver (who had replaced Hinton Bridgwater in the Edinburg sub-district), and 10 under Jimmy Poore at College Station.

In that fiscal year of 1962, for the second year in a row, the Texas District set another all time record in numbers of coyotes killed, with an astounding 34,754 total verified scalps sent in. But there were signs that the trappers' take would be going down. Compound 1080 had been used on a test basis for two winters, in the coyote factory of Dimmit, Maverick, and Webb Counties. The same number of trappers in those counties now took only one half as many coyotes as they did the year before. It seemed that Compound 1080 was going to make the difference.

The Edinburg sub-district was starting to compete with the San Antonio sub-district for great numbers of coyotes—Duval County came up with 3,865 coyotes scalped. In the same time period, the San Antonio sub-district total showed a drop from 9,312 to 8,125, probably reflecting the use of 1080 in a part of that sub-district.

In 1962, coyote control was financed by agreements with 217 of the 254 counties in Texas, by agreements with 46 "clubs," groups associated to finance their own predator control work; and with 44 individual ranches, who assessed themselves voluntarily. One of those ranches was the huge King Ranch, which occupied parts of five Texas counties. But some very small sheep spreads, places which probably ran about five hundred head of sheep or goats, also participated. The list of individuals contributing to predator control funds included Dolph Briscoe, who later became governor of Texas.

During the same year when Texas government trappers were scalping the new record of 34,754 coyotes, Compound 1080 was used very extensively in some parts of Texas. A total of 674 lethal bait stations were placed, bearing a total of 82,967 pounds of treated carcass material. That forty tons of 1080 meat was 79 percent consumed; another great number of coyotes died at a distance from the 1080 station. One can only guess the total number of coyote deaths caused by the predator control program in Texas during fiscal year 1962. I was there, and I would make an informed guess that the total exceeded 50,000 coyotes. I make this high estimate primarily because of the very good acceptance of 1080 station material in the southwest part of the coyote factory. Entire horses were consumed in one night of exposure, and second bait stations were similarly demolished. The following year's reduction in coyote take in those areas bears me out in this regard.

From 1909 to 1983, the coyote control program in Texas has been the first, the largest, and the best of all the cooperative programs in which the federal government has been involved.

Public support of the program has been steadfast in Texas, because the land is well suited to sheep production—if it were not for the coyote. The program started because Texas had so many coyotes that sheep ranching was not profitable. Despite the large and expensive predator control problem, the increasing numbers of coyotes taken in Texas point to one conclusion: the coyotes' numbers are growing. I believe that after over sixty years of war on the coyote, there are more coyotes in Texas than any other state of the Union.

Chapter 13

West Texas Vignette

The late Darwin (Shorty) Ivy worked for the old Predator and Rodent Control Division of the Bureau of Sport Fisheries and Wildlife and was the Assistant District Agent in Marfa. He rated the handle of "Shorty" and also rated his reputation as one of the most entertaining people I have ever hit the trail with. He could have been a wonderful stand-up comedian if he had ever wanted to be indoors that much.

Because of that sense of humor, "making a well-tee" with Shorty was one of the pleasures of my life when I was stationed in San Antonio. "Making a well-tee" is a corruption of the Spanish phrase, *"dar la vuelta"* which means to make a loop, or to take a turn around.

I rode the Southern Pacific to Marfa, and found Shorty impatient to be off. "We got a call from one of the good old boys ranching out northeast of here," he said. "He's got a coyote or two killing lambs at his place and he wants some he'p." I tossed my rifle and sleeping bag roll in the back of Shorty's truck, up against his famed all metal chuck box and we headed out. A word or two about that chuck box might be in order. Shorty Ivy had had the chuck box built to withstand all the hard treatment it was bound to get, with an overlapping lid to keep out water if, as Shorty put it, "It ever does rain out here." The box was lined with wood, an inch thick, to provide "nailing room" as Shorty put it, so that he could put in partitions and hooks. That box contained a few cast iron utensils—a small griddle, and a "tres-pes," the three-footed dutch oven that Shorty used most often if he was cooking. There were also some big cans with tight fitting lids for flour, sugar, and coffee, a small assortment of canned foods, plus sacks of beans and other staples. Shorty built this box to be indestructible. And it nearly was until Shorty drove his pickup up such a steep road that the "two ton" chuck box broke its moorings and came bouncing out. The chuck box bounced from boulder to boulder down the rocky road for fifty yards; then came to rest in the middle of the two ruts that served as a road. Shorty bragged that the box stayed in one piece, but it never was the same again. It couldn't be bent back into shape enough to fit the truck again. I guess that box might still be lying out behind Shorty and Glenna Ivy's place there in Marfa.

We got to the ranch in late afternoon and went to headquarters to visit a bit. We were told which band of sheep the coyote was working on and where they were located. "Must have a litter of pups som'eres," the rancher opined, "cuz she's killing every single day. I take it to mean she's feeding pups. Like to put me out of the sheep business if you don't put a stop to her."

We drove several miles across the sandy flats, heading for a distant windmill which marked the location of the big flock. At least a thousand bleating woolies dotted the land around the windmill. A lone cowhand snored in the sun, protected from the wind by the crumbling wall of an old sheep shed. He was embarrassed at being assigned to sheepherder duty. "I sure do hope you get rid of this "gyp" quick, Mr. Ivy, 'cuz I wa'nt cut out to be no damned sheepherder. Smell of the damned things likes to make me sick."

We searched for sign of the denning female, thoroughly checking a number of dry washes downwind of the flock's location. We found lots of coyote sign, but all of it was meandering—"hunting tracks" Shorty called it—as opposed to the "straight as a string" tracks made by the adults returning to the den with food. We found no straight tracks, nor did we find the den. We were at least fifty miles from any town that night, so we made camp right where we were, about a mile east of the windmill and the flock of sheep.

Shorty could use less firewood to cook a meal than anyone with whom I've ever camped. He used a square-ended spade to dig a trench, five inches wide, ten inches long, and less than four inches deep. In this ditch he started a fire of bone-dry mesquite over a tinder of dried grass and ancient cholla cactus ribs. When his fire was blazing nicely, he laid the cooking grate over the fire and put the coffee pot on. By the time the coffee had boiled long enough to float a horseshoe, the mesquite was only a patch of red glowing coals as big as your opened hand. Over that glowing mesquite Shorty cooked a good meal, liberally laced with chili-pitin, the tiny, volcano-hot round peppers. There was usually enough heat left over to warm the water he used so sparingly to wash the dishes.

When everything was again stowed in the big chuck box, we set up camp by the sun's fading light. Camp is perhaps too grandiose a word to describe our sleeping quarters. We rolled out bedrolls atop those old canvas and wooden army cots. We would have slept on the ground, but that country teaches you to respect rattlesnakes.

We hunkered down alongside the cots for half an hour while the final light died in the west. Shorty regaled me with stories of his explorations in Old Mexico south of the Big Bend National Park—twenty years earlier. The dry breeze began to stir a little, setting a biting edge here in this bone dry climate. "Time to hit the sack," Shorty allowed. I required very little urging. It had been a long day.

Snuggled into the bedroll, with a flap of canvas—a "wagon sheet"—doubled round me on the upwind side, I was warm and comfortable. I had started to drift off into slumberland when a coyote howled to the south of us. I saw Shorty sitting on the edge of his cot, slowly rolling a cigarette as he turned his ear to the south. As he struck the match, the coyote howled again, the long, quavering falsetto song that is so hard to locate. Ventriloquial in nature, the night song of the coyote is one of the eeriest sounds to be heard in the outdoor world.

Each time the coyote howled, Shorty would dramatically point toward the sound, then lower his arm and wait for the next howl. Three times he pointed to the southwest, then stubbed out his cigarette on the rocks under his cot.

"Think you've got a line on her?" I asked.

"That bitch better give her soul to God, because her ears belong to Ivy," he replied as he swung his legs back into the sack.

Before the night had yielded to the first false dawn, Shorty had roused me from my slumbers.

"We'll have time for breakfast later," he whispered, "right now we want to find a good calling spot before it gets light enough so she can see us moving around."

I followed Shorty westward for a quarter of a mile. A shallow depression in the prairie suited his needs and we took shelter in some sparse sagebrush while Shorty tested the light breeze with a wet finger. As soon as it was light enough to make out the crosshairs in a scope, Shorty nodded to me to get down a little lower. He began to call. The second agonized scream was still ringing in my ears when Shorty whispered, "Here comes the dog!"

The big male coyote was coming at a swinging trot from the west, across the light breeze. I began the agonizingly slow maneuver of getting my rifle barrel around to cover the target without being seen by the sharp-eyed animal.

"Don' be in no hurry; lessee if we can draw the gyp," Shorty whispered. Then he called again, much more softly this time. The big male shifted into high gear and came directly at us. He was running so fast that I could hear his paws hitting the hard ground!

My trigger finger itched as I watched the coyote grow larger in my scope. Suddenly Shorty swung his rifle up, and aimed in another direction. My coyote came to a skidding stop, hair standing on end as he saw Shorty materialize out of the sagebrush. I tightened my finger on the trigger and it barked at the same split second that Shorty's .270 bellowed.

I jumped up and looked at my coyote that was now just a crumpled bit of gray-brown fur against the side of a cactus. I swung the muzzle to the other side, where Shorty had been aiming, but he said, "Like I told you last night, her ears belong to Ivy." We scalped the two coyotes and turned to go.

"After breakfast," Shorty said, "we got our work cut out for us. There's a den out there somewheres with a mess of pups in it, and they deserve a better fate than to starve to death."

It was about 10:30 when we found the den, a big hole in the side of a shaky gravel bank. It would have been dangerous to dig it out—the banks might collapse on us. So we listened to the noise of pups inside, tossed in two gas cartridges, and sealed the entrance of the burrow with dirt. The pups died quickly and almost painlessly.

Chapter 14

The Den Hunters

The most damaging coyotes are usually the pair of adults who have the duty of feeding a big litter of pups. Unfortunately, that time coincides with lambing time on sheep ranches in most of the coyote range. For the coyote, the temptation of a sheep flock is greatest, and the opportunity is also the greatest. That lambs are slow and incapable of taking care of themselves is really unimportant, for a coyote is easily capable of catching and killing any animal in the flock, and doing so with ease.

To eliminate this threat, both adults must be killed, not just one of them. The surviving adult will continue to feed the young in most cases, and will probably double its slaughter of sheep, doing the work of both parents at once. Eliminating the young will also produce the desired result. When the pups are destroyed, the adults will (sometimes) stop killing sheep, because they no longer have to find so much food. They will go back to their first love—rabbits and mice.

These are the reasons for den hunting and destroying the young coyotes. If the government trapper is merely interested in adding to his total kill, den hunting is also attractive, as he can scalp as many as eight pups from one den, or—and it is not rare—many more if two females are denning in the same den.

The arguments for den hunting are economic, unsentimental, and cruel.

The arguments against den hunting are emotional, humane, and strong.

Those opposed to den hunting argue—"That poor little innocent coyote pup has never killed anything in his life, why should he be killed, just because he MIGHT, at some future time, be a threat to somebody's livestock? He has a right to live, doesn't he?"

Others say, "Not all coyotes kill domestic livestock. Some of them live out their entire lives killing rodents, taking their place in the web of life—why should we kill the pups? They haven't committed any crime?"

Obviously, both arguments are true and worthy of consideration. But the most persusasive of all arguments against killing coyote pups is that the pup is cute and appealing. Even the most hardened of den hunters feels a slight qualm when he knocks them in the head and cuts off their tiny ears. A fat, roly-poly coyote pup, tripping over his own feet, is appealing. Many people, seeing the coyote at this stage, fall in love with them and take them home for pets. Almost without exception, the coyote proves a treacherous, uncertain animal as a pet when it is full grown.

In some years, and in some districts, den hunting has produced record numbers of scalps. In others, it is only an incidental cause of coyote mortality. The difference is usually not in the nature of the terrain, but in the ambition, or lack of it, of the individual

Expert den hunter Tom Sparks with pups taken from a Texas Panhandle den, after a three-day search for the hidden den.

government trapper. Den hunting is hard and dangerous work. One man, digging out a den of coyote pups in Wyoming, was trapped in the den when a rock formation over the den collapsed. He survived three days, waiting for help to come. While trapped, he ate two or three of the coyote pups—raw.

Whether or not you feel that denning is acceptable—morally or ethically—the lore of the den hunter is interesting. How do you start?

First of all, find the general location the coyote is using. Listen for the coyote howls at daybreak and at sunset—that sound will give you your first clue as to a starting area. If you know there are coyotes out there and they do not howl when you want them to, try a siren! A siren will cause all dogs including coyotes in the vicinity to howl—probably because its note is unpleasant to their ears. This approach is so reliable that some researchers have used the siren-induced howl response as a measure of coyote population density. The howl response is compared with the previous year's response to indicate trends; although it will not give the researcher a quantitative answer to the question, "Any coyotes here?"

Heard coyotes howling? Then you know that they are in that section of land, within about a half mile each way. Remember that the howl is somewhat ventriloquial in character. It is difficult to determine the location of the howler with any degree of accuracy.

Find where the coyote kills have taken place. This will give you another indicator. This isn't foolproof though. We have seen coyotes leave their den, pass through the middle of one or two flocks of sheep, attack and kill a sheep in the third pasture, bring the carcass all the way back through the other flocks, and feed their young with its parts. We have also seen coyotes kill sheep within one hundred feet of their den. It is my opinion, not backed by any research results, that the cautious coyote usually does not attack livestock close to its own den. However, no rules of behavior are ironclad when you are discussing the extremely variable nature of the coyote.

After you have established the general territory you feel the den is located in, put on your walking boots and set out to search in earnest. Now comes the work.

Think about the terrain. Is there any one place which automatically suggests itself as a denning location? The banks of eroded gullies offer ideal places to start a den tunnel. Are there any gullies around your location? If so, look at the upper reaches of the banks, for the coyote is too smart to den where rushing waters can inundate the den entrance. Over most of the coyote's range, however, you won't find just one place which automatically suggests itself as a den. Most of coyote land is fairly flat, with no up and down banks.

Remember, too, that the coyote female seldom digs her own tunnel from scratch. Opportunistic as always, the coyote prefers to modify the existing tunnel made by a badger or some other mammal, changing it to suit her anticipated needs. Remember, also, that the female coyote will usually clean out more than one burrow when it comes near to whelping time. She may clean out as many as six. It is not known whether the female coyote does this as a necessity, ensuring that she will be near one or the other when her time comes, or simply to relieve nervousness about approaching motherhood.

Now, start looking for tracks. When you find a coyote track, follow it for a ways to see if it traces a straight line—as it will when the adult is returning to the den with food for the pups—or if it meanders, indicating the pattern of the hunting adult. Characterizing the line of movement as "direct" rather than as "straight" would be more correct perhaps. A straight line will not be followed if there is an *easier* way, such as the smooth cowpath through dense sagebrush. If the cowpath meanders, it still is the most direct route to the den.

The direct track you've been following offers your first line of position, for an extension of that line will lead to the vicinity of the den. Follow the track as far as you can—you may even be lucky enough to follow it directly to the den. If you lose the direct track, as I usually do, hunt for another. Follow the second direct track as far as you can. You now have a second line of position, for an extension of that line also leads to the den. Where would those two lines intersect? Roughly, at the den.

Sometimes a hunter must find as many as six lines of position leading to a den before actually finding the den. This happens when the burrow is artfully concealed, or is very small and partially concealed behind a slab of fallen rock, a spreading bush, or perhaps a kangaroo rat's nest. In some areas of very sandy soils, the den may actually not be a den at all, but merely a depression scooped out of the loose sand, exposing the pups to the elements.

Secondary burrows, those cleaned out by the female but not in use, may throw you off the track, for there is usually coyote sign at the secondary den also. Perhaps this is another reason the expecting coyote bothers with secondary burrows. As the pup-nursing time proceeds along, the female is apt to visit and revisit those secondary dens, for reasons best known by her. Do not assume that you have hit pay dirt, just because you have found a freshly dug den, with coyote tracks in the damp sand. This may be a secondary den.

You can usually hear the pups in a den, if you lie quietly with your ear close to the burrow for about ten minutes or more. The pups are playful and squeal as they tumble about, giving themselves away. If you don't hear anything after ten minutes at a den, the chances are very good that you have more den hunting to do.

Once the den is found, a lot of hard shovel work is required before you reach the pups. Be very careful. The threat of a cave-in is always present in most soils. A den of pups is not worth your life. Always work in pairs, so that one can rescue the other in case of trouble. Never go very far down into the ground; the danger is too great.

Most professional den hunters that I have known were always federal trappers. They wanted those coyote scalps, but most of them didn't want to lose their own in the process. If the den wasn't easily dug out, or "wired out" as described earlier, the government trapper tossed a couple of gas cartridges into the den and shoveled dirt to effectively seal the gases inside the den, killing the occupants.

Do you approve of den hunting and the destruction of the pups? Your answer probably depends upon whether or not you own sheep or goats!

Chapter 15

Aerial Coyote Hunting

Given the western sheepmen's virulent hatred for coyotes and the wide-open nature of western sheep country, it was inevitable that someone would suggest shooting coyotes from an airplane. The obvious advantage of excellent visibility, especially in winter when the coyote stands out from the white background like a false note from the Mormon Tabernacle Choir, coupled with high speed and the ability to search large areas in a short time, teased ranchers into trying it out.

Some pilots were trying aerial hunting as early as 1920. Almost simultaneously, private pilots tried their skills at getting within range of coyotes in the Dakotas, Idaho, and eastern Oregon. One of the most noteworthy earlier attempts was that of O.R. (Ole) Aslakson, of near New Rockford, North Dakota. Aslakson not only flew the plane, but did the shooting as well! He actually built his own plane, a Heath Parasol, from a kit, but never used it for hunting coyotes. He began serious aerial coyote hunting in 1936.

George Albrecht, North Dakota's famed Skywolf, killed 3,363 coyotes from the air between 1926 and 1949. He shot his first coyote from the air in 1926 as a gunner for Clyde Ice, pioneer pilot from Spearfish, South Dakota. In 1931 Albrecht shot a (then) record 113 predators in one winter, six more than Clyde Ice's 1929 record. Records were made to be broken, however.

Author Cadieux with some coyotes shot from an airplane in western South Dakota in 1958.

Another famous North Dakota aerial pioneer was Billy Snyder, of Bowman. He bought his first plane in 1928 and promptly went to work as a coyote hunter. He preferred the shooting to the piloting; or maybe he was just a better shot than most people ever hope to be. Snyder introduced a new refinement into the game by fastening a wooden grain door to the struts of the plane, then securely tying himself onto the grain door. This innovation allowed Snyder better visibility and unlimited firing zones, which are probably responsible for his unequalled record. The shooting platform didn't catch on because of North Dakota's low winter temperatures. At times Snyder came in to a landing so stiff from the cold that he had to be lifted off of his grain door bed.

Billy Snyder was so dedicated to his craft that he practised shooting at newspapers staked out on the bare plowing in the summer time, so that he could see exactly how his shotgun was patterning. At the age of 87, he was still an excellent marksman with the rifle and shotgun, and enjoyed hunting sharptailed grouse and Hungarian partridge across the fields of Bowman County.

George W. Kerr ran the Bureau of Sport Fisheries and Wild-life's Pocatello, Idaho, Supply Depot during the early years of aerial hunting. I asked him about the history, and his reply, a personal communication to me, dated March 30, 1982, is reproduced here in its entirety.

Pocatello, Idaho
March 30, 1982

Mr. Charles L. Cadieux
8209 Harwood N.E.
Albuquerque, New Mexico 87110

Dear Friend Charles,

Please excuse me for writing this in longhand, but I am now 82 years of age, have undergone three operations in the last two years and have arthritis so bad that I cannot use a typewriter. I hope you can read this. I do remember meeting you years ago and was pleased to receive your letter and to learn of your interest in the history of aerial hunting for coyotes.

As you mentioned, there were many private pilots who did some coyote hunting prior to Milton Robinson, but there is no doubt in my mind that he is the first Fish and Wildlife Service employee who officially inaugurated coyote hunting with aircraft on a professional and full time basis. Just to illustrate this, I might tell you that I got my private pilot's license in February of 1919 and occasionally did some coyote hunting for sport and fun during the 1920s. I knew a sheepman living in Boise who had several bands of sheep grazing on federal lands. He had the usual problems with coyotes. He also had a son about 18 or 19 years old so I suggested that they purchase a light plane and I would teach him to fly and maybe we could control some of the coyotes around his sheep. They bought a small pusher type aircraft with tandem seats and the engine mounted above the wing. The front seat of this plane was located right in the nose of the aircraft, making it ideal to shoot from. During the next two winters the boy and I did a lot of hunting around their bands of sheep and accounted for quite a number of coyotes. I merely mention this to illustrate that private pilots hunted coyotes in the early 1920s and gave me a definite interest in this method of control, and also some experience in it.

My present memory is not so good; however, I will give you as much information as I can regarding Milton Robinson. The Fish and Wildlife Service transferred Milt to Bismarck in 1942. By chance he met with a private pilot named Billy Marks who had a couple of small planes which he used for hunting coyotes. He not only taught Milt to fly, but he also had Milt to fly with him as his gunner. Another pilot by the name of Ed Schroch, a business associate of Billy Marks, was a pilot and quite often they would take both planes and hunt together. In 1944 Milt bought his own plane, a Piper Cub, and made arrangements with the North Dakota District Agent to use his plane for coyote hunting.

Authors Note: Milton Robinson had a long battle with his supervisor, Adolf Hamm, the man in charge of predator and rodent control work in the Dakotas-Nebraska District. Hamm was concerned that even the most careful of pilots might forget where he was while in the heat of the chase and fly right into the ground. Hamm knew that the plane had to come down to very low altitude to have any chance at killing the fleeing coyote. He also knew that the gunner had to use a shotgun, for the chances of hitting a coyote with the single projectile of a rifle would be very slim. Now back to George W. Kerr's letter.

I would therefore say that Milton officially inaugurated aerial hunting of coyotes for the Fish and Wildlife Serivce in 1944 in North Dakota. In 1947, Milt was transferred to the Idaho District with headquarters at Boise. The district agent there at the time was Lee Twitchell. He immediately arranged for Milt to use his own plane for hunting coyotes in various trouble spots throughout the southern part of Idaho. Lee Twitchell and a hunter named Bud Baler served as gunners.

In 1945, the U.S. Air Force declared a surplus of a large number of aircraft. I immediately contacted Dorr Green, who you will remember was chief of Predator and Rodent Control (PARC) in Washington and asked him if the supply depot could acquire three of the Piper Cubs and two of the larger planes. I don't remember what the larger aircraft were, but we got all the planes we asked for. When we received them it was immediately apparent that we could not use the two larger aircraft for our purposes. I flew one of the larger aircraft and found it too fast for our use. They had large Pratt & Whiteney 600 horsepower engines and their stall speed was far too fast for our use. About this time, the Game Management Division in the Alaska District was flying Grumman Goose aircraft. One of them came in for a landing at the Anchorage harbor and tipped over. When the hot engines hit the cold water, it cracked them. We took the engines from

94

*the large planes and sent them to Alaska to replace the damaged engines
in the Grumman Goose plane.*

*We used one of the Piper Cubs as a source of parts, cannibalizing
it to keep the other two running. As manager of the Supply Depot, I
made arrangements to rent the two planes to the various states PARC
divisions. The Idaho District rented one of our Piper Cubs. Milt sold
his own plane and started to use one of our Cubs. We rented it to the
Idaho District for twenty dollars per month. We paid all maintenance
and fuel costs and the Idaho District paid Milt's salary and expenses
and furnished their own gunner.*

*The first Piper Cub had only an 85 horsepower engine and we soon
learned that it was underpowered for the altitude, terrain, and low
level flying, so I traded it in for a new Piper Super Cub with the 125
horse engine. I flew with Milt several times and it was my opinion that
we needed still more horsepower. So after a couple of years I traded the
Super Cub in for another one with the 150 horsepower engine, the
biggest motor certified for the Super Cub. This plane proved very
efficient and we have twice replaced it with newer Super Cubs, each one
with the 150 horsepower engine; all have proved very efficient machines
for coyote hunting. We have remodeled the left windows of each aircraft
to afford better shooting angle, position and visibility for the gunner.*

*In about 1960 Don Heath started flying shotgun for Milt so Milt
taught him to fly. When Milt retired, Don took over the flying and
has flown ever since. Don has now accumulated more than one thousand hours.*

*Charles, I hope you don't have too much trouble reading my writing,
and I apologize for the length of this letter. But if it gives you the
information you asked for, I will be content."*

*With kindest personal regards,
George W. Kerr.*

As we have seen from George Kerr's letter, Milton Robinson
secured permission from the conservative U.S. Fish and Wildlife
Service to use the airplane technique. The method was immediately successful when tried under the right conditions: (a) smooth
and unbroken snow cover, (b) light winds or still air so the plane
could maneuver safely at low altitudes, and (c) good visibility.
Good visibility does not always mean bright sunshine. Even covered with very dark glasses, the glare off of new snow can be too
much for most eyes.

The technique was simplicity itself—just cruise the area where
the coyote is thought to be, flush him out, and shoot him. Sounds

simple, but not always! At first the coyotes were naive and would trot off a short distance and watch as the plane approached. When they turned to run at the last minute, the gunner fired. Most of the successful gunners that I've known claimed that they gave the running coyote a negative lead—they fired behind the coyote to compensate for the fast forward motion of plane and gun. Other gunners claimed that they fired right at the coyote, and because both types of gunners regularly scored, it must be interpreted that no two shooters see the sight picture the same.

In later years coyotes became very wary and escaped by diving into deep brush and lying still. If the pilot and gunner were skillful enough to locate the coyote in the brush, they still had a hard time flushing him into flight again. When he did start to run, the average coyote would take a straight line until the plane got close. Then he would dodge quickly to one side or the other. Gunners found that the coyote usually dodged twice, then tried to outrun the plane on the third approach.

I tried aerial hunting with Walden Lemm as pilot, out on the flat lands of Harding County, South Dakota. I missed badly the first few times. Walden threatened to hit the next coyote with the wheels if I missed again. I finally connected on a three-shot barrage from my autoloader and got a tremendous cheer from the three government hunters, all expert aerial gunners, who were watching from the ground.

I never saw Milton Robinson shoot, but I've heard that he was very good. Mark D. Worcester, who later became a district supervisor, was also a skilled gunner from the Dakotas. Mark recently told me that he once killed fifteen coyotes in one day, in Golden Valley County, North Dakota. "Nothing to brag about," declaimed Mark, "they were so thick that you could get fifty to sixty chances in a day when I first went out there to work." Mark illustrated the coyote situation in western North Dakota by telling me of a young ranching couple who kept a constant watch over a flock of ewes ready to start lambing. The sheep were in a pen close to the house. These two vigilant ranchers took turns guarding the sheep around the clock. For some reason or another, they relaxed their vigilance one noon, and accepted an invitation to lunch with a neighboring couple. They were gone forty-five minuts and returned to find 43 ewes killed in broad daylight by coyotes—but none were eaten.

Mark had an easy time finding coyotes when he was first stationed in Beach. In the first twenty days he shot sixty coyotes with the rifle from the ground. He simply drove slowly, looking for coyotes, and shot from the edge of the road. It was very easy to use the aircraft against such a dense coyote population. It was also very expensive compared to other techniques. The federal government decided that aerial tactics must be used selectively, only taking the plane out after a known killer. Aerial hunting could not be used to reduce the overall numbers of coyotes in an area.

Cecil Albers of Spearfish and Ralph Block of Faith, South Dakota, were excellent gunners when flying with Walden Lemm. Lemm never let the excitement of the chase lead him into a tactical error. When maneuvering at fifty feet off the ground, one tactical error is apt to be the last tactical error. Lemm and the gunners once sighted a bunch of coyotes that were hiding in a tall, but sparse, stand of sweet clover surrounded by level fields of snow covered stubble. There were six coyotes hidden there. When the plane made the first buzzing run, three of them bolted out of the far side, intent on putting miles between themselves and the plane. They were about thirty feet apart and literally running for their lives. Walden swung after them and added a bit of throttle as he neared the running targets. Cecil Albers fired once, twice, three times—and three coyotes lay upon the white snow. Walden turned tightly and gained altitude to go back to the clover patch. One of the remaining three was spotted, already three hundred yards from the shelter and heading in the opposite direction. The gunners swung in on it . . . fired once, then twice, and the coyote somersaulted on the hard-packed snow.

That left two of the six and Walden had to do some very low-level flying to move those two—which turned out to be adults. The other four were nine month old pups, young of the year. The two adults dodged and turned, but stayed inside the sweet clover. After the third pass failed to dislodge them, Walden sideslipped in as slow as he could and Cecil fired at the shadowy figures half-hidden in the clover. This stung one or both of them, for they suddenly bolted out of the north side and headed for the shelter of the creek bottom brush, half a mile away. Walden swung around in close pursuit and the plane overtook the running coyotes. I heard the shotgun once, twice. Then the motor revved up again and I heard it slow down before the shotgun barked once, twice, and the third time.

"All right, you guys," the CB said, "Scalp those six and I'll go see if there are any more."

That was a very happy rancher who viewed the six dead coyotes that afternoon. "They'd just started to kill lambs," he said. "Took four already, and I sure would have had hell without you guys. With that plane they ain't got a chance, have they?"

As far as I was personally concerned, the coyotes had a better than fifty-fifty chance when I was manning the shotgun. First of all, I had a problem with airsickness when the plane did a lot of tight turns near the ground. The nearness to the ground doubled the effect of relative movement and my gastric awareness was might high. On those rare days when I conquered that problem, I still couldn't visually pick up the running coyote fast enough to get into position for a shot as we overtook the running target. As mentioned before, Walden threatened to hit the coyote with the wheels if I missed one more time. I'm sure he wouldn't have tried, because he was a very careful pilot—but I bet that he could do it if he tried.

Aerial hunting was natural for some areas of the Dakotas, eastern Montana, Wyoming and eastern Colorado, as well as parts of Kansas, Oklahoma, and farther west in eastern Oregon and southern Idaho. Aerial hunting was totally useless in the areas that had the thickest population of coyotes—the mesquite and prickly pear jungles of central and southwestern Texas. There, it was not possible for the pilot to follow a dodging coyote as he ducked in and out of clumps of heavy cover.

Inevitably, someone would have an accident with this type of aerial hunting—sooner or later someone would fly into the side of a hill while chasing the dodging coyote. Bill Pfeiffer had such an accident in North Dakota and there was another one in New Mexico. There might have been others.

Another view of the early history of aerial hunting was provided by Weldon Robinson, who headed up Control Methods Research for the Denver Wildlife Research Center for many years. He sent me a copy of a 1944 report put out by the Dakotas-Nebraska District. That report says that assistant district agent Howard Marley "had an opportunity to interview Clyde Ice who hunted predators by plane in western South Dakota . . ."

In a personal communication to me, Weldon Robinson adds the information that "Clyde Ice was aerial hunting coyotes in 1927. He is the earliest of the aerial hunters I know of. He is now 93, hale and hearty, and lives in Pinedale, Wyoming. Clyde was a significant character in the early days of aviation."

The 1944 Dakotas-Nebraska report states that the Fish and

Wildlife Service personnel cooperated with three North Dakota plane hunters by helping obtain ammunition and permission to hunt over certain areas. In return, the three pilots kept records of their kill and costs, and made this data available to the Fish and Wildlife Service. In 848 hours of flying time, aerial hunters killed 511 coyotes and 831 (red) foxes between November 1 and March 31. They also estimated that 10 percent of the coyotes and 15 percent of the foxes seen escaped. The most popular plane was the Piper Cub. They estimated the cost at $8.00 per flying hour as follows:

Pilot salary	$3.00
Gunner	1.00
Depreciation & maintenance	2.00
Gas, Oil and storage	1.50
Shells	.50
Total	$8.00

Don't those price figures make you yearn for the "good old days?"

How effective was the airplane as a means of killing coyotes? Rew Van Hansen, animal damage control chief for the Fish and Wildlife Service in Pierre, South Dakota, tells me—

There are no official records as to who shot the most coyotes. To give some idea as to the potential, one service individual shot 97 coyotes in four hours one afternoon from a fixed wing aircraft. Another shot 77 in two hours. Both of these incidents immediately followed winter storms and heavy snow. There were several reports of 70 to 75 coyotes taken in a day's hunting and I am sure that these would be considered high for normal hunting conditions. The Piper Super Cub was the plane used in all these operations, to the best of my knowledge. Some higher numbers have been taken by helicopter. These exceed 100.

Russ Strait of Albany, Oregon, reports that in southeastern Oregon he piloted the aircraft that took over 90 coyotes in one day.

Aerial hunting is still used to control coyotes that are known sheep killers. It is the most effective, and the most selective of all the control methods. Selective, because the aerial hunter goes to the spot where the killing occured and starts hunting from that point. He thus greatly increases his chance of bagging the offending coyote. Costs have certainly soared since the good old days, however.

The most effective and selective of modern control methods—helicopter coyote hunting.

Chapter 16

The Coyote-getter

It looks harmless, but it is a deadly form of coyote killing. I refer to the *Humane Coyote-getter,* ™ developed by Fred Marlman, which became operational and approved for government use in 1939.

The one coyote-getter that was used for several decades consisted of a hollow aluminum tube, like those used for electrical conduits, pinched together at the bottom end to make a sharply pointed stake. At the other end was fastened an ingenious spring mechanism holding a .38 caliber revolver case. The case was loaded with a tiny amount of gunpowder and a small amount of powdered cyanide.

In use, the trapper put a metal rod inside the hollow case and hammered on the rod to drive the stake well into the ground. Then he put the loaded and cocked mechanism into the top of the stake, being very careful not to put his hand over the top of the getter. Then he wrapped the top of the getter in a piece of foul-smelling rag or sheep's wool. This foul-smelling rag attracted the coyote. When he decided to find out what was making the scent, the coyote would grab the getter with his mouth and pull upward. This upward pull released the firing spring mechanism. The firing pin hit the primer, the primer exploded and fired the small bit of revolver powder, and drove the powdered cyanide out through the top of the getter into the mucous membrane of the coyote's mouth and throat.

This is all that shows above ground of the efficient coyote-getter which propels powdered cyanide into the mouth of the coyote curious enough to mouth the foul-smelling rag wound about the top of the machine.

With the poison injected directly into the blood stream death came very swiftly for the coyote. He usually ran off less than one hundred yards; then dropped dead.

The advantages of this method of coyote killing should be easily apparent. Because of the fetid odor of the lure, it attracted only canines. Therefore there was no threat to the bobcat or mountain lion. Black bears were attracted, and they did pull the getter upon occasion, but the cyanide charge was not strong enough to kill such a large animal.

Because the getter was fired only by an upward pressure against the odorous lure, it was not discharged (at least, not often) by the hooves of livestock. One large, and ham-handed government trapper in south Texas used to show off by firing the getter with his hand, palm down to absorb the cyanide charge against his calloused paw. I saw him do this several times, with apparently no ill effects. Then he got hold of a getter which evidently must have had a bigger explosive charge in it. The poisonous wad hit his palm with such force that it raised a painful blood blister. That was the end of that silly trick.

When the first caveman started using a club, he probably told his fellows that this weapon was so effective it would make them "king of the hill" for all time to come. The same thing happened when the lance was developed, and the bow and arrow, and the atomic bomb. None of these weapons have provided dominance very long. Either the other guys got the same weapon or they developed a system for negating its effects. All the weapons man has developed to fight the coyote, with the one exception of Compound 1080, have brought similar consequences.

In a talk given to the Sheep and Goat Raisers of Texas, way back in 1955, Cedric R. Landon, the respected chief of predator control in the Lone Star State, reported that during the first year coyote-getters were used in Texas, they accounted for 76 percent of all coyotes killed. Traps counted for only 24 percent. Six years later, the number of coyotes taken with coyote-getters had dropped to 60 percent, and steel leghold traps accounted for 40 percent. A certain percentage of coyotes did become "getter-shy," but the getter continued to take a substantial part of all coyotes killed in the U.S. for nearly forty years.

The U.S. government secured the rights to the coyote-getter from its inventor and started production of the mechanism and the specially loaded .38 shells at its Pocatello, Idaho, supply depot in the year 1939.

As a result of agitation that the coyote getter posed a danger to non-target species, the Fish and Wildlife Service began experimenting many years ago with a device which used only the spring mechanism to expel the powdered cyanide, rather than the explosive charge. This experimentation resulted in the M–44 coyote getter in 1969. With the exception of the propelling mechanism, the M–44 and the *Humane Coyote-getter*™ are almost identical. Today the federal government uses only the M–44.

Frank Martin was one of the foremost practitioners of the art of the coyote-getter. He was stationed in the brush country of southwestern Texas, where coyotes were thicker'n the fleas on a coyote pup. In 1961, he was engaged in a tight competition with a neighboring trapper to see which one could scalp the most coyotes in one year. Frank had more than four hundred coyote-getters set along ranch roads in his area when the year began. He would rise very early in the morning and start his rounds. All getters were placed where he could see them from the seat of his pickup truck. When it got light enough to see, Frank was well on his way. If the getter had not been fired, he didn't get out of the truck, but drove on. If it was fired, he jumped out of the truck, reset and re-scented the getter, then circled around to find the dead coyote. Scaping off the two ears with a bit of connecting skin, he jumped back in the truck and went on to the next stop.

Frank had several things going for him in his attempt to set a record. He could remember the location of every single coyote-getter, which saved a lot of time on his rounds. This ability was all the more remarkable when you consider the nature of his territory—a sea of mesquite and prickly pear, with very few landmarks of any kind.

Secondly, he had some ranches to work that had not been worked for the two previous years of high coyote population. This gave him a very large pool of coyotes, that had not become getter-shy.

Thirdly, and most important, although he certainly didn't get paid for for it, he worked from "can to cain't" as they say in that part of Texas—from the time he could see until he could no longer see. He also worked about six and one half days each week during the busiest months. At several points during the year, I made a few rounds with Frank, just to see how he was acquiring such a bale of coyote scalps every month. I decided that, more than anything else, he did it by dint of hard work. At the end of the year, Frank's total was 2,714 coyote scalps—verified by actual count performed by Pat Cordova at the PARC warehouse in San Antonio. I believe that all but a handful of these coyotes were killed by coyote-getters, and the great majority of them were taken on two or three ranches! Strangely enough, after removing three thousand coyotes from a single Texas county, it was still possible to take coyotes on the getter there! This certainly indicates that there was a considerable migration into Frank Martin's territory.

The ingenuity displayed by trappers in concocting their various getter scents was boundless. The more sickening the odor, the more attractive it seemed to be to the coyote. Beaver castor, mink musk, oil of anise, rotted fish were favored ingredients of the more successful scents. Most trappers carried their scents in tightly lidded Mason jars, for obvious reasons, and most of them used a small paint brush to smear the concoction on the getter. Not all, however! I shall never forget one of the trappers in west Texas who must have been completely without a sense of smell. He commonly smeared the scent on the getter with his bare hand, then wiped his hand on a rag, and laid the rag on the seat. I was with him on his rounds one cold day. The cab was tightly closed with the heater going. The results were beyond description!

Experimentation went on all the time, as trappers vied to produce a more enticing scent. One effective mixture that worked in western South Dakota was simple to make. You simply put half a quart of dead frogs in a quart Mason jar, punched two or three holes in the lid to let the gases escape, and placed the jar in the bright sunlight until the flesh melted off the frogs bones and there was left only a liquid, or semi-liquid, paste. Coyotes found that irresistible; humans found it sickening.

Another South Dakota trapper used a bit of scented powder puff that once enhanced the aroma of a lovely lady. The perfume was delicate, but the coyote nose is very sensitive. The trapper reasoned that they might like a bite of that perfume. It worked! But it worked better on red foxes than it did for coyotes, so the trapper quite using it.

Naturally the getter was deadly on dogs, as well as wild canines. In fact, it worked better on domestic dogs because they lacked the native caution of the coyote and fox. Pressure from hound dog men forced many county commissioners courts to prohibit the use of the getter in their county, which severely curtailed the effectiveness of the weapon. Hell hath no fury like a hound dog man who has lost his dog to a coyote-getter. Federal regulations required that every property with coyote-getters on it had to be plainly marked with orange warning signs which said that the getters were there and warned to keep dogs out. But every year there were dog losses. This aroused much enmity for the coyote trapper.

Chapter 17

The Leghold Trap

It is impossible to determine who made the first leghold steel trap, took it out, and proved that it would catch and hold an animal. But it is known that steel traps in some form or another have been part of the American frontier ever since the first settlers moved westward into the new lands.

Every boy who has experimented with the "figure four" method of rigging a bait so that its removal dropped a box on the unsuspecting varmint has daydreamed of making a living with a bundle of traps. They conjure visions of "mountain men"—traps slung over their shoulder as they head for the beaver country. Like most young men who grew up in rural areas, I cut my teeth on the small varmints and added a few dollars to my scarce "spending money" by trapping muskrats. A muskrat was easily taken by a trap set on a half-submerged slanting log, with a bit of carrot fastened artfully above it so that the 'skrat had to stand on his hind legs to reach the bait. When the trap snapped shut on his leg, he dove into the safety of the deeper water but drowned under the weight of the small trap.

I graduated to trapping red fox and coyotes—or at least, trying to trap them. I found the coyote to be the most trap shy creature in Stutsman County, North Dakota, and I never succeeded in taking a single one in my #2 traps. Many times they were sprung, but no coyote. In retrospect, I know that the tired old

Typical steel leghold trap in the hands of a skilled trapper is still very efficient.

#2's simply couldn't hold a coyote. I didn't own a bigger trap, and although I studied the *F.C. Taylors* trap catalog religiously, I never found a #3 or #4 that I could afford.

Steel traps are perhaps the single most reliable method of killing a particular coyote, if the trapper knows what he is doing and is willing to spend the time and the effort required to fool the cautious coyote. Any #3 or larger *Newhouse* or *Victor* trap will hold a coyote, if the trap is in good condition. After watching experts set traps from North Dakota to northern Mexico and from Louisiana to western Utah, I have picked up a smattering of lore that distinguishes the real trapper from the beginner.

A few generalizations, please. The northern states trapper is more apt to use a trap stake, driven into the ground to hold the trap and chain from departing for parts unknown when the jaws snap shut on the leg of a coyote. The southern trapper is more apt to use a drag—usually a piece of concrete reinforcing rod, bent to form two fishhook ends. The drag is buried entirely, usually below the trap itself. If buried to one side, the chain and drag must be camouflaged as carefully as the trap itself.

Baits are not used on the trap itself, except by amateurs. Baits should not be positioned directly on the trap itself but in such a spot where the coyote will spring the trap while reaching for the bait. If a bait is placed on the ground, over the trap pan, a coyote will carefully pick it up, without snapping the trap.

Instead of a bait, the experienced trapper places his trap where he thinks the coyote will have to step, and then takes pains to make sure that he does step right there. Artfully placing a big stone, a piece of wood, or a clod of frozen dirt, he makes it logical for the coyote to step where the trap is. However, that same experienced trapper knows that he's better off not disturbing the natural appearance. All wild animals have a "new object reaction," a cautious approach to anything new. The coyote has learned that a change in the environment can mean danger, and he reacts accordingly. This is just one reason why a trap is more apt to catch a coyote in the second week it is placed in a particular position than the first week.

The very best set, in terms of results, is placed in a slight depression dug in the earth. The removed dirt should be placed upon a canvas trap cloth during the setting operation. The trap must be solidly bedded against solid ground, so that it will not tip without being tripped. When the trap is solidly in position, the loose jaw is lifted and a "trap cloth" very carefully placed over the pan and the tripping mechanism. For best results, this "trap cloth" should be a piece of very old, very sun-dried, soft canvas. I remember some very successful trappers who kept that soft canvas in a bed of very dry sheep droppings, to neutralize any "man smell" it might have picked up from the trapper's hands. The trap cloth keeps dirt from interfering with the tripping mechanism.

Trap, drag, and cloth in position, the trapper sifts a very thin layer of dirt over everything to completely hide the trap. This is a critical part of the operation. If too much dirt is used, the coyote's foot won't spring the trap. If too little dirt is used, the trap will be evident—in outline at least—and that is enough to warn off a clever coyote who has had experience with traps. If the dirt used is too damp, it will freeze into a hard clod and prevent the trap from functioning properly. If it is too dry and too light, it will be blown off on the first windy day. The fact that the trap is in a slight depression helps keep the dust cover in position.

A bobcat will usually make a few frenzied attempts to pull loose and then sit quietly, waiting to see what will happen. Not so the coyote. He will desperately try to escape and will keep on fighting the trap as long as he has strength to continue. Coyotes occasionally do "wring off," twisting their leg around and around until the tendons snap and the bone breaks. The great numbers of peg-legged coyotes which dot the literature of coyote trapping are evidence that traps do break leg bones and allow the coyote to twist off, or even to gnaw its own bones and tendons to get loose.

To stop the "wringing off" loss of coyotes and to make trapping more humane, the U.S. Fish and Wildlife Service has long experimented with "trap tabs." Trap tabs are filled with a quick acting poison, usually cyanide. Customarily, when the coyote finds itself held by the leg, it attacks this thing that has hold of it. He bites viciously against the steel trap, into the cyanide capsule and dies quickly. This method has been surprisingly effective and is a good refinement of the age-old steel trap.

Offset jaws on coyote traps have also reduced the loss of coyotes to "wringing off" or to broken leg bones. These jaws give just as solid a hold, but they do not meet in the middle. The leg bone is held securely, but is not broken by the snapping shut action of the trap. Offset jaws are now standard with almost all professional trappers.

There have been many other attempts to make the trap more humane. One of these, the *Havahart*™ trap, tries to entice the animal into a box-like metal structure that closes behind him and holds him, unhurt, until the trapper comes. The coyote, though, is simply too cautious to enter this trap. Another attempt at humane trapping is the *Conibear*™ trap, which has wider steel jaws to snap shut against the body of the animal, striking an almost instantly killing blow. These are more difficult to set than the old steel leghold trap; they are costlier, are very heavy and cumbersome in sizes big enough to handle a coyote. They have never been well accepted by coyote trappers, although they have done a good job on smaller furbearers.

The biggest factor in humane trapping is the frequency of the trapper's visits to the trap line. If he visits all of his traps every day, usually just eyeballing them with binoculars from the window of his car, he will come upon the trapped animal in time to put it out of its misery. If he visits the traps only every two or three days, an animal may die of thirst, or simply exhaustion from fighting the trap, before the trapper gets there. It is also true that it is not economically profitable for a furtrapper to visit all his traps every day. Trappers are currently much more concerned about their public image than they have been in the past, and this concern is reflected in more humane trapping practices.

A coyote caught in a leghold trap quietly awaits its fate.

Several organizations have waged war against the steel leghold trap for the past ten years, seeking legislation which would outlaw such trapping. Some of these organizations are composed of individuals who are genuinely motivated by humane concerns. These are definitely deserving of respect. Other organizations are motivated only by concern for the salaries of their leaders. These last organizations use an issue such as the obvious cruelty of trapping to generate more funds, and have not demonstrated any real concern for the wellbeing of the animal. It is very difficult to distinguish between the real tears and the crocodile tears shed by certain organizations.

These organizations can be separated into the good ones and the ones dedicated to raising dollars only. It is a case of actions speaking louder than words. For example, several years ago the New Mexico herd of desert bighorn sheep was infested with a severe outbreak of scabies that was causing the death of many individual desert bighorn sheep and threatened the very existence of the herd. The only known cure was a costly program of trapping the animals, treating them with chemical dips to kill the scabies, and isolating them before releasing them back into the wild. Inasmuch as state game and fish departments are not able to raise great sums of money outside of the budgetary process, the New Mexico State Fish and Game Department asked all conservation organizations for help in paying the costs of this humane program to save wildlife from suffering and death. Not a one of the so-called humane organizations came forward with as much as one thin dime to help pay the costs. That tells us something.

As to the position of steel trapping in the overall coyote scheme, C. R. Landon put it rather well, way back in 1955 when he made a report to the Texas Sheep and Goat Raisers Association. He said, "It is the consensus of experienced predatory animal hunters that the old reliable steel trap is the best single tool at his disposal. Our records for the last eighteen years reveal that steel traps have accounted for more predators found and scalped than all other methods combined." This statement was made ten years after the introduction of Compound 1080. It is also noteworthy that he made the distinction, "found and scalped" rather than simply "killed." Coyotes killed by Compound 1080 are seldom found.

Agitation to ban steel leghold traps continues. From year to year there is a concerted effort to introduce and pass such legislation in U.S. state assemblies. Such legislation has an increasingly better chance of enactment as our population becomes more urban and less rural. As we get farther and farther away from our pioneer beginnings, such tools as the steel trap seem destined to join the ax and the muzzleloading rifle as mementos of the past, rather than suitable tools of the present.

112

Chapter 18

Compound 1080

When sodium monofloroacetate was perfected in the early 1940s, it was hailed as the best, most species specific, most fool-proof predator poison ever developed by man. When President Nixon signed the executive order in 1972 to the ban the compound from federal lands and federally-supported programs, it was the most feared poison ever turned loose on the coyote range of the west.

History reveals that Compound 1080, and only Compound 1080, has ever succeeded in reducing the numbers of coyotes on a given range to 5 percent of what it had been before that poison was used. Opponents of Compound 1080 claim that it kills every kind of meat-eating bird or animal that comes onto the same quarter section with the poison. Where is the truth? As usual, it lies somewhere in between the widely differing views. Let us establish a few facts.

There is no known antidote.

The chemical itself is a finely grained white powder, which is soluble to a very marked degree. Put a tiny bit of the white powder on top of your fingernail and watch it. It will slowly change character as it absorbs moisture from the air. First it will turn into a mass like wet sugar, then it will totally disappear! It actually dissolves into the moist air. This solubility is one of its most striking features—both a plus and a minus.

Compound 1080 is odorless and, as far as we know, tasteless. This is very important, as there is no warning factor, no stimulus to any of the senses which might warn the animal consuming a 1080-impregnated bait that there is more here than just the meal. After twenty years of use in the old Branch of Predator and Rodent Control, many of us, however, felt that there was some kind of a warning factor—some kind of immediate reaction caused by the chemical—so that the coyote did not ingest as big a meal as he would have under normal conditions. This is not a hard and fast statement—we only "thought" that there was some kind of warning factor. We had no proof. In fact, we also saw some coyotes actually gorge themselves upon 1080-treated meat, consuming as much as ten pounds of the treated meat, so that their stomachs were distended.

Compound 1080 does not produce a "pretty" death. It works on the nervous system so that the vital processes are speeded up —as if the motor had lost its governor, and unregulated, ran itself to destruction. Typically, a 1080-killed coyote will end up lying on its side, all four feet going through very rapid running motions as it finally dies. Compound 1080 does not kill quickly, either. Unlike strychnine, which causes a very few sharp convulsions and then quick death, 1080 dooms the animal to several hours of agony before it finally dies.

Because it dissolves so quickly and completely, 1080 is a very lethal way of killing rats. Pans containing a 1080 solution are exposed in a locked building overnight, and picked up in the morning to prevent other animals and children from drinking the solution. In a normally dry environment, it is unbelievably effective. This method cannot be used against coyotes, because it would endanger every other life form that drinks water.

Compound 1080 was used for the control of coyotes in range country in the following fashion: a bait animal (typically an old, low-priced horse) was killed and cut up into eight or twelve parts. While the meat was still very warm, a water solution of Compound 1080 was injected with a "brine gun" that featured a long needle with holes along its sides. When the handle was pushed on the brine gun, the 1080 solution was injected with considerable force into the warm meat. If done properly and quickly after the death of the bait animal, the poison spread very evenly through the entire meat portion.

Then the meat was allowed to set for eight to twenty hours to stiffen up and to seal the edges so the poisonous solution would not seep out of the meat. The individual pieces were then trucked to the bait station location. Permission in writing was obtained from the landowner, of course. In fact, the landowner customarily furnished the bait animal at his own expense. Once at the chosen site, warning signs were posted to notify all who could read that a poisoned bait was exposed there, and all dogs should be kept away.

Then the meat was tied to a tree or to a heavy stake. Heavy wire was used to secure the bone section, so that coyotes could not pick it up and carry it off.

Warning signs were posted at all the entrances to the field or pasture in which the bait was exposed. Each bait station was carefully plotted on a map. When the season was over, the bait station—or whatever was left of it—was carefully picked up and destroyed. Only two methods of destroying the bait remnants were approved—burial in a deep hole, such as an old abandoned mine shaft or a well, and burning. Burning was the most common method where I worked. We commonly saved up old tires to incinerate the bones.

Typically, coyotes would not feed on a warm bait station. I believe they were warned away by the remaining human scent. There were exceptions, of course. One night in Maverick County, Texas, a large fourteen hundred pound horse was butchered and treated. The eight portions were left on large branches, to allow air to circulate under them overnight. We came back in the morning, expecting to pick up our eight baits to be placed at prescribed locations around the county. But the entire horse had been eaten and the bones gnawed! We found more than a hundred dead coyotes in the surrounding chapparal that day.

If the horse bait was properly treated, two or three good bites of the treated meat was enough to seal the coyote's fate. When the poison began to take effect, the coyote became extremely nervous and excitable and often took off running at high speed. He seldom died near the bait station, and often died more than half a mile away.

In the earliest days of Compound 1080's use on the northern plains, there was considerable experimentation with the so-called "heart injection" method of treating a sheep carcass. Sheep seemed to be a natural choice as a bait because coyotes commonly fed upon them. Later experience proved that the horse was a far better bait animal. In the heart injection method, a live sheep was injected with red-tinted 1080 solution by means of a pressure needle, directly into a large artery. When a bit of pink began to show in the lips of the sheep, the injection was stopped and the sheep killed. Often, the sheep dropped before time to kill it— perhaps a victim of a stroke caused by the added fluid under pressure.

During those years, a whole sheep carcass treated with Compound 1080 was placed at a coyote station very near to the boundary of an Indian reservation in North Dakota. The government trapper who placed it, and the accompanying warning signs, then went on to place six other sheep. He returned the same way that he went in, some four hours later. He stopped to look at this first sheep station and found it missing!

With fear and trepidation, he followed the tracks in the snow to a nearby Sioux Indian village. There he lost the tracks. He went from door to door in the village, telling all who would listen that the sheep was poisoned with a deadly poison and that it would kill any person who ate even a bit of the meat. Then he went to the Bureau of Indian Affairs and asked for help in spreading the word that the sheep would kill humans if eaten, and dogs if the carcass was thrown away. Despite their best efforts they were unable to find any trace of the sheep.

A week later, one of the Sioux told what had happened. They had stolen the sheep. Since it was still warm, they were certain it wasn't spoiled. The carcass was skinned and the sheepskin tacked up on the wall of an old building to dry. They cut the mutton into small pieces and put the whole works in a big kettle of water to boil. When it was completely cooked, they poured out the water and at least eleven people ate parts of the sheep. None of the Indians even got a stomach ache. But six dogs died after licking the fluids that ran down the wall from the sheepskin!

The only explanation for the sheep dinner not affecting the Sioux is that all—or nearly all—of the active ingredient had been dissolved out of the meat during the boiling process and then poured off. The ultra-soluble 1080 had bonded with the boiling water, not with the meat. No other explanation was available, and we'll really never know as no one will volunteer to repeat the experiment.

The early effectiveness of Compound 1080 as a coyote killer is almost beyond exaggeration. Seventy pound bait stations were cleaned up in a week. A second fifty pound station was added. It was cleaned up in three weeks. A third forty pound package lasted through the rest of the winter. In the spring one or two active dens would be found in the area—where in the preceding year fifty active dens had been found! Like every other control method, Compound 1080 did not get every single coyote in the area. There are always a few coyotes who will not get any of the carrion bait—for reasons that we do not yet understand.

Opponents of 1080 and they are legion, claim that Compound 1080 is an indiscriminate killer, destroying all of the carnivorous life forms exposed to it. The proponents claim that 1080 is very specific for canines and felines. Further, because few felines eat carrion, it is almost entirely restricted to the canines. "Keep your dogs away," claim the 1080 backers, "and we'll kill only coyotes."

Not so, claim conservationists on the other side of the issue. Russell W. Peterson, the widely respected president of the National Audubon Society, issued the following statement about efforts on the part of the state of Wyoming and the National Woolgrowers to have 1080 put back on the list of permitted predacides:

> Before the ban (on 1080) the fortunes of the woolgrowers had been declining for decades for reasons largely unrelated to predation: foreign competition, development of synthetic substitutes for wool and, in many cases, inefficient management practices. The sheep raising business has continued to decline for these reasons, and coyotes continue to be the scapegoat for the industry's problems.
>
> There is no convincing evidence that the ban on predator poisoning has led to an increase in coyote predation. The U.S. Fish and Wildlife Service has found that the coyote population has not exploded, as alleged by the sheep ranchers. Moreover, most coyote "controls" have remained in effect; some seventy thousand coyotes are still trapped and shot annually by the Fish and Wildlife Service, and an estimated two hundred thousand additional coyotes are now taken each year by fur trappers.
>
> Past experience with Wyoming and other states shows there is no way to curb the indiscriminate use of 1080 no matter how restricted or supervised its use is supposed to be. Widespread abuses prevailed in Wyoming and elsewhere before the ban. Enforcement was almost nonexistent. Federal field agents living in wool growing communities were under too much peer pressure to resist bending if not breaking the 1080 restrictions. Even after the ban, in the winters of 1975–1976 and

117

1976–1977, the Wyoming Department of Agriculture defiantly put out carcasses laced with Compound 1080.

Legalizing 1080 for coyote control will neither eliminate the coyote nor improve the wool growers fortunes. What it will do is poison our public rangeland and needlessly destroy wildlife. Its use is economically unsound and ecologically idiotic. No substantial evidence justifying the 1080 use existed in 1972 when this poison was banned; none existed in 1978, when EPA refused to permit a return to predator poisoning, and none exists today.

There is only one item in the above statement by Mr. Peterson that I wish to take issue with—now—because I can give first hand testimony. My statements can be used as evidence as they are not second hand, nor hearsay. They are my personal observation. That item is the statement that "Enforcement (of the 1080 regulations) was almost nonexistent." That is definitely not true. I put in six years of enforcing those 1080 regulations, and Mr. Peterson, I did my damnedest to enforce them. I succeeded, too. I can also speak for a dozen other supervisors in the old Branch of Predator and Rodent Control, because I know from personal experience—not from hearsay—that they also did their damnedest. But I should not interject my personal views here. Let's stick to facts.

Opponents of 1080 say that it results in wholesale death to non-target species. I have heard this argument countless times. When I ask for proof, I get only a vacant stare, or the mumbled reply, "Anyone knows that it will kill all other animals!" It sounds like something to worry about, and if 1080 did result in increased mortality of non-target species it would be something to worry about. Let's stick to the facts.

The treated animal bait, as used by the Fish and Wildlife Service, was prepared by injecting 1.6 grams of 1080 into 45.4 kilograms of bait. At the Denver Wildlife Research Center, scientists set out to discover how much 1080-treated bait was needed to kill 50 percent of those individuals (of a given species) that ate the bait. The results of long and intensive scientific experiments are summarized in *Special Scientific Report—Wildlife No. 146,* still available from the Superintendent of Documents, U.S. Government Printing Office, Washington, D.C. 20402 (Stock Number 2410-0284).

The most striking result published in this scientific report is this: at least 50 percent of coyotes that eat 1.4 ounces of properly

118

treated bait will die (LD_{50}); the average bear would have to eat 102 ounces of the same material to cause the same (LD_{50}) percentage of deaths in the bear population. A badger would have to eat 13 ounces of the bait, a Golden eagle would have to eat almost a pound of the bait, and a turkey vulture could safely consume as much as three pounds of the bait. The complete tabulation is printed as follows:

Average weight and amount of properly treated coyote bait (1.6 g. of 1080/45.4 kg of bait material) that selected species must consume in order to obtain a median lethal dose (LD_{50})

SPECIES	LD_{50} mg/kg	Average weight lbs.	Amount (oz.) of bait consumed to reach LD_{50}
Coyote	0.1	30	1.4
Cat (domestic)	0.2	3	0.3
Fox	0.3	12	1.6
Bobcat	0.66	22	6.6
Bear	0.15–1.0	300	68.0–136.0
Mink	1.0	3	1.4
Marten	1.0	3	1.4
Magpie	0.6–1.3	0.5	0.1–0.3
Badger	1.0–1.5	19	8.0–13.0
Golden Eagle	1.25–5.0	7	4.0–15.9
Turkey Vulture	20.0	6	54.0

I was surprised to see that the badger can be killed by 1080, for I have seen badgers set up housekeeping right under a horse carcass bait treated with 1080. A South Dakota badger stayed there all winter long, exhibiting a strong territorial defense of his turf—the horse carcass. He was observed feeding on the 1080 treated horse during the winter, and was still there—and quite angry with us—when we removed the last of his guaranteed free lunch in late March. In Texas, I have seen signs of opossums feeding on 1080 bait stations but have never found a dead opossum in the field that could conceivably be listed as a victim of 1080.

I have heard tall tales of secondary poisoning as a result of 1080 bait stations. In six years of studying the situation in the field in North Dakota, South Dakota, Nebraska, Texas, New Mexico, Colorado, and Wyoming, I have never seen any signs of secondary poisoning related to a 1080 bait station. That doesn't mean that it could not have happened, however. In fact, the scientists who wrote the *Special Scientific Report—Wildlife #146*, claim that it can happen. The report states that—

"Secondary poisoning can occur with sodium monofluoro-acetate. However, Gal et al. (1961) have shown that rats can metabolize sodium monofluoroacetate to non-toxic metabolites, and/or excrete a large amount of sodium monofluoroacetate and fluorocitrate prior to death, if the dose is approximately an LD_{50} (up to 32 percent of a 5.0 mg/kg dose of sodium monofluoroacetate excreted). In addition, sodium monofluoroacetate tends to exert an emetic action, especially on canids which have ingested more than an LD_{50}; thus, a portion of the toxic material may be regurgitated. These features can result in a portion of the poison ingested by an animal not being present in the animal at death. In any event, due to dilution, the concentration of sodium monofluoroacetate in the body of the victim will be much less than in the bait itself. Therefore, an animal feeding on a sodium monofluoroacetate victim is much less likely to receive a lethal dose than from feeding on the treated bait itself, even if the animal feeds on the internal organs and their contents, the portions of the victim with the highest concentration of sodium monofluoroacetate and/or its toxic and non-toxic metabolites.

The Golden eagle, an animal that normally consumes the internal organs before other portions of its food, demonstrates the reduced hazard of acute poisoning via secondary sources. To obtain an LD_{50} of sodium monofluoroacetate from a secondary source such as coyotes, a seven-pound Golden eagle would have to consume the internal organs of from seven to thirty coyotes killed by sodium monofluoroacetate—assuming the coyotes ingest an LD_{50} and do not excrete, detoxify, or regurgitate any of the toxicant and that as in rats approximately 40 percent of the dose is present in the internal organs at death. The internal organs of a coyote account for approximately 20 to 25 percent of its live weight, or six to seven pounds. A Golden eagle's daily consumption of food equals approximately 30 percent of its live weight, or two pounds. As noted previously, animals can metabolize and/or excrete continued small doses of sodium monofluoroacetate without succumbing.

Since regurgitated material is actually only partially digested bait it presents a possibility of primary poisoning. This vomitus, however, is quite finely divided in comparison to the 1080 stations, a condition which speeds the decomposition of the vomitus and speeds the leaching of the sodium monofluoro-acetate into the soil."

Russell W. Peterson joins an illustrious group of mistaken people when he wrote that 1080 would "poison our public rangelands." There is absolutely no basis in fact for this ridiculous assertion. In fact, Saito (et al.) analyzed water from streams in a sodium monofluoroacetate treated area for five months following the application of sodium monofluoroacetate rodent bait and did not detect a trace of the chemical. The *Wildlife Report #146* continues,

> Horiuchi demonstrated that fluoroacetate breaks down in the soil. David and Gardiner demonstrated that both sodium monofluoroacetate and fluoroacetamide break down in the soil, and concluded that there are no apparent reasons for condemning the use of these compounds because of a buildup of toxic residues in the soil. Sodium monofluoroacetate either exhibited no measurable toxicity at all or exhibited no measurable toxicity within two weeks, depending upon the soil type, when applied to soils at ten parts per million, and exhibited no measurable toxicity within eleven weeks when applied to soils at fifty parts per million.

The controversy over the question of using Compound 1080 against coyotes has generated a surprising amount of smoke—but almost no light on the subject. If rampant emotionalism could be eliminated from the discussion, and a decision based only on provable facts, rather than secondhand hearsay evidence, a consensus in the environmental community as to whether or not to use the predacide 1080 might be reached. Lacking such a rational atmosphere, the current controversy shows little signs of solution.

In the long history of man versus coyote one fact remains: only Compound 1080 has been able to measurably reduce numbers of coyotes and maintain that reduction over a period of several years.

Whenever government trappers used poisons, all entrances to the area were clearly posted with warning signs. Here District Supervisor Calvin Johnson posts a Texas gate.

Chapter 19

Strychnine Drop Baits

The coyote was a full grown male, its coat as prime as a west Texas coyote ever gets. It carried its bushy bottle-shaped tail low. Its sharp nose constantly read the message of the wind; its keen eyes moved unceasingly over the terrain ahead; its alert ears listened attentively for the slightest sound. This never-ending vigilance had kept the coyote safe for six years—ever since his mother had snapped at him, driving him away from her late in the fall of his first year.

He had lived nearly six years in Irion County, halfway between Ketchum Mountain, a 2,730 foot hillock, and the breaks of the Middle Concho. He had learned that men were dangerous, and had easily kept out of sight in this big ranch country where mankind is a seldom visitor. This coyote had no enemies— though Golden eagles had swooped playfully at him that very morning, driving him scuttling into the taller brush where the eagles couldn't maneuver. Nothing had really threatened his life or safety. There were many rabbits, many kangaroo rats, half a dozen varieties of mice, and big flocks of sheep within easy distance. The sheep furnished him a big meal whenever he wanted one. The sheep were never herded, they were simply turned loose to feed on the gravelly, sandy hills—without any protection against the coyote. There were few coyotes in the area that year, and the loss of lambs was not significant in the huge operations of that district.

The coyote was heading for an easy meal this evening: three dead sheep whose carcasses lay near the corner fence of the big pasture on the McMahan Ranch. He hadn't seen the dead sheep; they were more than half a mile ahead, but his nose had already told him that there were three animals lying there—each with its different odor or stage of putrefaction. He knew that they were close together, perhaps within ten feet of each other. He also knew that they were very dead and so there was little need to hurry. If another coyote were to reach the carrion before he did, he knew he could simply drive the other coyote away. This coyote was the alpha male of the area then, and hadn't faced a serious challenge from another coyote for two years.

Because it was ingrained in him from the gifts of heredity, he did not drop his native caution as he approached the carcasses. His expert nose brought him a side tidbit of scent—the smell of a small bit of meat which lay to the side of the track. He approached it warily, nose stretched out ahead, his slim, pointed face aimed right at the small bit of meat. There was a bit of man scent, which caused him just a split second of concern, but it was old human scent and not very strong. It was like the human scent on the gate, which the rancher had to get out of his pickup to open. That scent was a normal part of life on the coyote's territory, and did not frighten him.

But the enticing smell of fresh meat came to him from that bit of meat. Loud and clear it gave the message that here was a "something good." He sniffed the morsel again, then snapped it up, gave it a flip back into his throat and swallowed it. He went looking around, sniffing carefully for more of the meat. He found a tiny scent trail which told him that the meat had "rolled" to its location, but that was meaningless to him now. The strong scent of the dead sheep was the main signal coming on his data line, and his nose computed the distance to that meal as being less than three hundred yards. His nose also brought the somewhat disturbing message that another coyote was already feeding there. That message was only slightly disturbing, because his nose also told him that the other coyote was a young female, one he had met and sniffed noses with many times. She posed no threat. When he approached, he expected that she would trot away a few hesitant steps, then assume a subservient posture, and sidle back to the meal; her every motion showing that she wanted only what he did not want to eat.

Quickening his pace, he trotted to within fifty yards of the dead sheep. Suddenly an excruciating pain stabbed him in the stomach! In surprise and anger he whirled around, trying to bite himself in the stomach, trying to reach that stabbing pain and hurt it back. Again and again the pain shot through him, stiffening his thin body in convulsive spasms. Then he yawned, his mouth gaping open, stiff with the agony of the biting fury within him. He fell, staggered to his feet, fell again, kicked feebly a few times, and lay still.

The strychnine had done its work neatly and quickly. The total time from ingesting the meat until the first pain was only seventeen minutes. From the first spasm of pain until death, the clock's minute hand moved only three minutes.

Two days before the coyote found the strychnine in the morsel of meat—called a drop bait—two employees of the U.S. Fish and Wildlife Service had led an old horse out to an isolated part of the ranch pasture and killed it with a single shot from a twenty-two pistol aimed in a line from left eye to right ear. Expertly, with razor sharp butcher knives and the skill born of long practice, they "roped" the meat, cutting it into long ropey strips of muscle, about an inch and a half in diameter. As they removed each strip from the carcass, they hung it upon a barbed wire fence to dry. The drying process was critical, for it had to be timed to make a hard crust on the outer surface of the meat, yet not so dry to make the inside of the meat less flexible than it had been before. Some seven hundred pounds of horsemeat was treated in this manner.

The men went to a nearby *pila,* to wash their hands and forearms free of horseblood and to drink copiously of the water that the windmill pumped from the ground. They ate their lunch after they had cleaned up, and stretched out in the scant shade of a mesquite for half an hour, then went back to finish the work. One expertly cut the meat into inch and a half squares. As he cut each piece, he flicked it expertly with his knife onto a flat wooden platform—part of an old door from a boxcar used in shipping grain.

On the flat working surface, his partner expertly spilled strychnine tablets from a shiny tin can, separated them, and cut each tablet in half. His knife point delicately sliced into a bit of meat, making a pocket. With the knife tip he picked up the half a tablet and pushed it into the pocket in the meat. He gave the bait a final squeeze to shut the mouth of the opening. The strychnine was in place, ready to be placed where the coyote would find it.

It was nearly sundown when the two men finished their job.

They had converted the tired old horse into about seven hundred pounds of drop baits. They very carefully cleaned up around their work area, and made sure that no poison was exposed in the pickup bed. The drop baits were secured in locked pails—formerly five gallon paint pails with solid lids each secured by a strong padlock—and set on the pickup bed. They covered the load with a tarpaulin, tightly laced down to prevent anyone from easily getting into the drop baits, and bedded in at a motel in Big Lake.

The next morning half of the load went west with the neighboring government trapper, and half of it stayed with the local man, who promptly began placing the baits. At every site, he went to the rancher and reminded him that they had signed a cooperative agreement authorizing the placement of poison baits on the ranch lands. He also discussed his general plan for placing the poison baits, describing the little-used roads which he intended to drive and the various waterings where he would place the baits. The government man also joked with the rancher about keeping the dogs close to home, because many a rancher had lost his pet simply because he refused to believe that the family pet would roam that far from home. "Keep 'em tied up for two weeks," warned the trapper, "or you'll lose a worthless lap dog!" The rancher chuckled, "He can't whup a coyote anyway, so I don't think he dares to go far from the home place. Might get picked on by them coyotes."

He drove the side roads slowly and carefully with the pails of baits on the seat beside him. He watched for coyote tracks. When he found them, he tossed out three or four baits about twenty feet apart. When he found droppings on the road, he placed drop baits carefully to one side of the path or the other, so the coyote would smell them as he passed that way again. Hidden baits, under a cow chip, or in the shadow of a bush, would surely be found by the coyote with his sensitive nose, but would be relatively safe from other animals that find their food by sight. The man had a lot of hard work invested in those baits; he wanted them to go to the coyotes, not to the smaller carnivores or raptors that shared the habitat with the coyote. He knew that he would kill many badgers, skunks, raccoons, crows, and smaller hawks because strychnine is not species specific. It kills a broad spectrum of meat-eaters.

Insects sometimes ate the baits, devouring them completely before the coyotes found them. The insects usually just ate around the white patch of strychnine, because even to the dung beetle or ant, it was very bitter. The strychnine dried in the wind and blew away as powder, no longer a threat to any form of life.

The sharp-eyed vultures found many of the baits, but incredibly, very few of them died from ingesting the strychnine.

Probably eleven hundred baits were in the local man's share of the drop bait supply, and he placed all of them in one long day of driving over the McMahan and surrounding ranches. For the next five days, he patrolled the area, trying to note where his baits were picked up. When he was sure that a bait was gone, he got out and walked the sandy lands looking for the dead animal. When he found a coyote, he cut the ears off, with a thin strip of connecting hide between them, and put them in the back of his pickup truck. He would send these scalps to San Antonio, to be counted by Pat Cordova and his assistants. The government hunter who sent in the ears would receive credit for the kill.

Seventy two coyotes were killed by the strychnine. How many others were killed and not recovered, no one would ever know. Bobcats were not affected, as they seldom eat carrion; but more than two dozen skunks were found, their bodies contorted in the typical strychnine death posture; seven raccoons—strangers in this almost treeless land; and sixteen badgers. As far as the rancher was concerned, this kill of smaller predators was simply an added dividend. "Good riddance," was his only comment when told of the kill of other species. He was, naturally, elated at the high number of coyotes killed.

In many instances, draw stations were used to bring the coyote to a particular area. A very ripe dead horse or cow was used as a draw station, and drop baits were placed in a circle around the draw station in the hope that the coyote would find the bait on his way in to check up on the draw station. Sometimes a completely dry cow skull is still a good draw station, as all of the coyotes using the area still come to the skull to use it as a scent station and to sniff it to find out which one of their coyote brothers has also been there, what health he was in, where he was going, and how long ago he had been there.

Using strychnine drop baits has been one of the tools of the coyote trapper ever since 1925 when it was used in the few government sponsored programs. It is just one of the tools, however, and there are always some coyotes that are too smart to pick up a drop bait. I have never known drop baits to eliminate all of the coyotes in any given area; but I have often seen them eliminate 60 or 70 percent.

Here's expert coyote caller and expert rifleman Frank R. Martin, in full camouflage and breaking his silhouette against a corral post as he calls the wiley coyote.

Chapter 20

Calling to the Gun

No two callers blow a predator-attracting call the same way. But that's no problem; no two coyotes respond to the call in the same way. I once had the opportunity to watch and hear an excellent coyote caller in operation. He was working a big rocky side slope to the Magdalena Mountains. I was well above him, watching and listening and not taking any part in the operation at all. In fact, he didn't know I existed.

He walked quietly, moving across the wind for about half a mile from where he had parked his ancient pickup truck. It was just getting dawn and he did not use a light. He moved quickly, keeping low and being very careful not to silhouette himself on any of the ridges. When he reached a bunch of uprooted tree roots that broke his outline but allowed unlimited visibility over all of the slope below and to both sides, he waited for a full five minutes. Then I saw him check his rifle, making sure that there was a round in the barrel and that the sights were clear. He removed the glove from his right hand, and put it into his pocket. He laid the rifle across his lap, and held it with trigger finger on the trigger. He slowly moved his left hand to his mouth and sent the "dying rabbit" call out over the cathedral-quiet of the New Mexico mountain morning.

The agonized scream wasn't very loud, for he wanted to take any coyote that might happen to be close. He waited for a long minute. I searched with my binoculars the approaches to his stand, watching for the coyote that we both hoped would come. A second long minute went by, without any movement from the hunter or the coyotes. Then the caller slowly raised his left hand again and this time the long, quavering scream came out much louder, strong and sustained, trying to get the message across that there was a small animal in great distress, a quick and easy meal for the opportunistic coyote. I adjusted the field of view of my 8 × 50's to put the caller in the center and waited.

He saw the coyote long before I did, for I saw a slight tensing of his shoulders through the glasses that gave him away. I moved the glasses slightly upward and saw a coyote coming full tilt, head up and alert—no attempt at secrecy, no stalk. This was a coyote that had heard the dinner bell and was making sure that no other meat-eater beat him to the free lunch. He came at full gallop, jumping over small bushes and dodging around cactus stands in his haste to get to the dinner table. He ran to within twenty feet of the caller, who suddenly rose up out of his concealment like Phoenix from the ashes. The coyote put on the brakes and skidded on all four. If an animal can have a look of amazement on its face, that coyote looked amazed. He didn't have time to turn and flee before the bullet caught him in the boiler room. The caller walked down to pick him up, carried the very dead coyote to a sharp pointed rock formation that would serve as an easy mark to find, then hurried eastward where the rising sun was just peeking over the rim. He walked another quarter of a mile, then took another good spot and called, exactly as before. This time I was glassing the country far to the north of him, far down slope. As the sobbing scream of the dying rabbit echoed across the *malpais,* I saw a coyote come up out of the *cenisa* and stare intently toward the caller. The caller never budged a hair. Both waited.

When the first minute had gone by, the hunter very slowly and carefully brought his hand up again. Again the long quavering scream rang out. I watched the coyote. Its ears shot up in astonishment. It listened to the full scream; then, without hesitation, the coyote wheeled around and took off, running as fast as it could get away from the caller.

The only explanation is that the second coyote was an adult that had heard the call before with frightening results. The lesson took with this animal. But it doesn't always take.

In southeastern New Mexico one day, I called a coyote from about half a mile away. He came up to within fifty yards of me.

I should have shot then, but I wanted him as close as possible. The "close shot" gets to be an obsession with most coyote callers. He came closer, but he also caught a whiff of human scent on the shifting breeze. He wheeled and took off out of there—but fast. I fired three shots at him. All three shots showered him with bits of gravel and rock, but missed. That coyote ran back the way he had come; stopped on a ridge three-quarters of a mile away and sat down to look back at me. I was out of sight when he looked back. Just because hope springs eternal in the human breast, I tried the call again—low and subdued, a rabbit in its final death throes. The coyote carelessly came toward me—on the run. He came to within one hundred yards; then a very tardy memory caught up with him. He stopped, and I shot. Got him.

I have seen coyotes come at a dead run to the gun, even when the caller was standing in plain sight and shooting! Even while the loud report of a high calibered rifle echoed from crag to canyon, the coyote still came to the dinner he had heard about. But don't count on it.

I started calling coyotes and red foxes in South Dakota in 1954. Most of the more successful callers then used a call which produced a thin reedy call, like a cottontail with its foot in a steel trap and a coyote approaching. That thin reedy call was fairly high-pitched and it worked. But I think it worked better on foxes than it did on coyotes.

Then I moved to the coyote factory of the world—Texas. When I used my thin, high-pitched call, I struck out. I then went calling coyotes with the late Hinton Bridgwater, who used a much coarser, lower-pitched sound. I said, "That damned thing doesn't sound like a rabbit." "No," Hinton allowed, "more like a Spanish goat with its foot caught in the swinging gate." I don't know that much about goats, but I do know that the coarse sounding call was much more effective on coyotes in Texas.

My first call was a tiny, cigarette-shaped and cigarette-sized call made by S. V. Higley, if memory serves me right. I don't think it is available any more. Hinton's call was homemade, a bit of bull horn with a brass reed fastened to it with one tiny screw. Most Texans used homemade calls, and most of them worked. Some of them worked because the caller was good at his craft; others worked simply because there were so damned many coyotes within hearing that they tried to outrun one another to get to the free meal.

One of the most successful callers was my good friend Byrl

Bierschwale. One morning in Uvalde County he and I took up positions ten feet apart, each of us hiding behind big prickly pear cactus. When Byrl sent out the invitation to lunch, three coyotes came on the dead run, really racing to get there first. I had the only gun. Byrl was strictly concentrating on calling this time. To make matters worse, I had a single shot rifle—a .22/250 built on a Mauser action. The first coyote was upon us almost before I saw him, and I swung the rifle like a shotgun and fired once at the blur of red and gray as it went by me, heading for Byrl. As the shot rang out, Byrl stood up. That coyote whirled and stared at both of us, as I fumbled trying to slip another round into the breech. The other two coyotes came into view at thirty feet. They stared at both the stationary coyote and the two excited men; then all three of them lit out of there.

"Dang, Mr. Chuck. I thought you was going to let those coyotes eat me up!" Byrl had a justifiable complaint. I hadn't held up my end of the situation.

The coyote coming to a call is not the "hunted"; he is the "hunter." The look in those lemon yellow eyes as he comes looking for a dying small animal, intent on killing is amazing. Once you've seen it, you're apt to be a converted coyote caller from then on. There is something very exciting about being the hunted, about completely fooling a clever animal. And, it's easier said than done.

Odie Roberts, calling coyotes near the Big Bend of Texas, had a gray fox come in to the call, coming so fast and so quietly that Odie didn't notice his approach. Well-hidden, Odie tried another invitation on his call. The running grey fox homed in on the sound, jumped into the rude blind, and bit Odie on the wrist, inches from the source of the sound. The grey fox didn't even break the skin. He whirled and got out of there so fast that Odie didn't even get off a shot.

A federal trapper out west, named Lyons, appropriately enough, once brought in a mountain lion when he was calling coyotes. I'm glad that didn't happen to me; for I still remember the shock when I was calling coyotes in Nebraska's Sand Hills and a bobcat came up to within ten feet of me, and sat there, just staring at me. I turned to go and looked into the bobcat's eyes. He left—I was too surprised to shoot!

Figuring that the young javelina must be a natural food item for a Texas coyote, George Schacherl and I tried an experiment. George had two baby javelinas as pets. As long as they were kept together, they were quiet and peaceful. Separated, they both set up an unearthly racket, lamenting loudly enough so that the whole world knew about their troubles. Somewhere east of Eagle Pass, we carried the pair of javelina shoats in a cardboard box out into a known coyote pasture. We picked our position carefully; then separated the two little pigs, who went into their singing act.

Eagerly we waited, rifles at the ready. Something moved out there in the prickly pear and tall grass. Then suddenly the area was overrun by about fifty full grown javelinas, all searching for the youngster in trouble. Snorting and popping their teeth, the little porkers charged around in the brush until they came too close to us, got a whiff of man-scent, and took off for parts unknown. Maybe coyotes don't take many baby javelinas? Maybe the community defense put up by the javelina herd scares off the marauding coyote? In any event, after many trials with the "live decoy"—baby javelinas, we had never called up anything but a herd of javelina. That happened twice.

If you want to try your hand at calling coyotes to the gun, here are a few suggestions.

1) Buy a call and a record of instructions. Learn how to make the right sounds.

2) Dress in camouflage clothing, add grease paint to your shiny face, and wear a hat with enough brim to shield your glasses from the reflections that will give you away to the sharp-eyed coyote.

3) Get permission from the landowner on whose land you will hunt.

4) Leave your car at least four hundred yards away from the calling site. Don't slam the doors or drive in with headlights swinging over the territory you expect the coyote to be in. Walk quietly to the calling spot, staying low and out of silhouette range.

5) Wait to call until you get your breath back and are not puffing. It will surely improve shooting accuracy and sometimes action comes very quickly after you call.

6) Blow softly at first, so as to entice, but not alarm, any coyote that happens to be close.

7) Wait five minutes, moving nothing but your eyes.

8) Call again, louder and longer, for twenty seconds.

9) Wait.

10) Try once more, loud and long. Wait five minutes. Give up and move on to another spot to try again.

11) Do most of your calling in the hour each side of sunrise; that's thirty minutes before and thirty minutes after. Also in the last hour of daylight.

12) Never blow your call while in plain sight. The last thing you want is for the coyote to equate the call with a human being.

13) Don't overhunt an area. If you call more often than once a week, you'll find the coyotes getting very wise. If you shoot in a spot, rest it for two weeks after the shot. This does not apply to areas where coyotes are very thick—in those spots anyone can call a coyote and kill it.

14) Best time of year to call—if numbers of coyotes killed is your criterion—is from February through June, when the pups are out and about and they haven't yet learned to be wary of anything and everything. If you want to sell the skins, of course, the schedule is different. Better stick to December 1 through March 15.

Don't give up too easily, wait until a coyote has had time to come a full mile, traveling slowly and carefully. Then wait a bit longer. Before you stand up, take a long, slow look around—you may have an audience that you didn't know was there. If you do, it will be triggered into instant flight by your movement.

If you want to kill coyotes most effectively, carry both a 12 gauge shotgun and a varmint rifle with a scope on it. The shotgun is for the fast action that takes place when you do your job perfectly and the coyote comes all the way in. And I mean all the way! The rifle is for the longer range shots.

Watch the area upwind and across wind from your hideout. Don't expect the coyote to come from downwind—none of them are that dumb. In some cases, coyotes will circle to get downwind of the caller. When they do that, it's all over, you aren't going to score from that position. However, if you are working with a partner, this can be turned to good advantage by placing the second rifleman downwind, well-hidden. This strategy will work best in the open country where you—and the coyote—can both see quite well. It won't work in the thick brush or where the coyote can approach in cover, giving you only a swift glimpse of his hurrying hide.

Outwitting a coyote with a call is a particularly satisfying achievement. You know that you have duped a slick character.

Expert rifleman Elonzo G. Pope, of Lubbock, Texas, once set a Texas record—insofar as I know—by calling up and shooting

When a coyote comes to the call, he is the hunter—you are the hunted, and his eyes look different.

seventeen coyotes in one day by himself. Many a Texas caller has brought up seventeen coyotes in one day, but collecting those seventeen coyotes with a rifle is an achievement to be proud of.

When I worked in the Lone Star State in 1961, to be exact, I witnessed another calling incident. Red Nunley owned a ranch that had not been worked with any measure of coyote control for several years. It was lightly hunted during the deer season, and held a tremendous number of whitetails and an unbelievable number of coyotes. Mr. Nunley wanted the deer, but not the coyotes, so he asked for a 1080 station. We got the necessary agreements signed and went about the business of placing the Compound 1080 station on about 44,000 acres of prickly pear and mesquite ranch country.

Byrl Bierschwale and I helped the resident hunter treat a big horse carcass. When we had finished the work on an isolated part of the ranch, we left the treated meat, as was our custom, to "set up" and get a crust on it so that it could more safely be transported to the eight different locations where it would be offered to the hordes of hungry coyotes. We finished our work about ten o'clock one sunny winter morning, left the meat, and headed on to other jobs. On the way out, we spotted two coyotes near the road and decided to take a crack at them . . . with Byrl doing the calling. Because it was the wrong time of day, because the coyotes had seen us, because we made no serious attempt to be quiet, none of us thought that we'd successfully call in a coyote. In the spirit of "it can't hurt" to try, the three of us got into the box of the pickup truck. I squatted at the rear, rifle at the ready, the trapper squatted near the cab, and Byrl sat atop the cab, in plain sight, and started to call.

Results were phenomenal. Nine coyotes came a-running. I got one, Byrl got two, and the trapper—using a trapline .22 rifle! —expertly killed three! Six dead coyotes in less than three minutes!

Thinking that we had run into a special race of coyotes that were unbelievably naive and innocent, we tried calling at two other locations on the road out to the main highway. Both times we took considerably greater pains to do the job right. We had the same caller using the same call.

We got zero results. Not a single coyote came to the call.

But they do come to the call often enough to make this one of the most exciting of all rifle hunting sports. You are the hunted, they are the hunters. This change-about lends an entirely new dimension to coyote calling.

Coyote hunting with dogs.

Chapter 21

Sight Running Hounds Against Coyotes

Probably one of the most expensive ways to kill a coyote ever devised is the system of using sight running hounds to overtake the prairie yodelers. Huge Irish Wolfhounds, capable of bounding twenty-four feet at one leap, are simply too much for any coyote to contend with in a sprint. Lean greyhounds, whippets, salukis, and many others of the long legged breeds have proven themselves to be immeasurably faster than the coyote—*in a sprint*!

These big dogs are very expensive to purchase and even more expensive to feed. They eat everything that doesn't bite them first, and it takes a lot of food to satisfy those long, lean bellies. About thirty years ago I had the privilege of accompanying some Nebraska ranchers on a coyote hound caper. On my first hunt I noticed a big chicken wire enclosure on the back of an ancient pickup truck. One side was rigged with releases so that one good yank on the rope would drop the whole side off of the crate. When the side dropped off, six long, lean hounds vaulted out and were off-and-running after whatever moved in the immediate area.

Usually the hounds had already sighted the coyote before the humans saw it. Their sudden excited yelping was the sign that coyote was on their menu—and in sight! But when we saw the hidden game first, and pulled the side off, the hounds often milled uncertainly for a second or two, searching for their quarry.

1. *When the coyote is sighted by the driver, he pulls a rope which drops the side panel allowing the dogs to pour out.*

3. *. . . quickly outdistancing the terrified coyote.*

140

2. *The hounds sight their fleeing quarry and give chase . . .*

4. *The lead dog tries for the throat, but the coyote dodges once or twice . . .*

5. . . . but the coyote has no chance and is quickly killed.

6. The Death of a Coyote.

Once the coyote is motionless, the hounds have no more interest and move away.

After they picked the coyote up, they were off in that unbelievably fast, ground-eating gait of theirs. Once when we spotted a coyote which was hiding, and loosed the dogs, they were totally lost. They pranced around helplessly, eyes searching for their quarry, but unable to scent that quarry even when it was as close as ten feet. If they were less than three hundred yards away when they spotted the coyote, that coyote was doomed. With incredible swiftness they closed the gap, probably traveling four hundred yards while the coyote made one hundred. The fastest dog drives in for the throat of the terrified coyote, which dodges—evading the hurtling dog and prolonging its own life by half a second. The second fastest dog then nails the coyote or forces it to dodge the second time. That second dodge usually is a dodge right into the speeding jaws of another dog.

Coyotes are brave *in extremis*. Often the tiny wolf wheels with lips pulled back, teeth gleaming in what he hopes is his most threatening pose. The fastest dog hits him and bowls him over. Before the coyote can right himself, the pack is upon him. Death comes quickly, though I must confess that I don't know the exact cause of death. These hounds never seemed to rip the skin, or to mangle the carcass in any way. They simply hit with a sickening snap of long jaws. The fleeing coyote is trapped under the jaws of the rest of the pack. Then the big dogs would prance around, looking off in the distance as if to say, "Well, what are we out here for?" None of the hounds seemed to have any interest in the motionless carcass.

On another occasion in southwestern North Dakota, the owner of the dogs got bored when we couldn't find a coyote to course. He loosed the hounds after whitetailed jackrabbits, and the dogs caught the jacks in about fifteen bounds. Actually, the rabbits gave the dogs more trouble than a coyote would have, as they dodged more eratically. However, like the coyote, they had no chance at all in a speed race, and their frantic dodging only prolonged the chase from thirty seconds to one minute.

I was amazed at the speed of these dogs and made the overly generous statement, "Why, these dogs can catch anything in the world!"

"Nope," said the rancher.

"What can't they catch?" I asked.

"Maybe get a chance to show you," he replied.

I had forgotten that bit of conversation when we headed for home in the late afternoon. There was no snow on the ground, and the flat prairie stretched off to the highest place in North Dakota, White Butte. We were jouncing along, talking it over when a young pronghorned antelope buck stood up within fifty yards of the road. The rancher reached around to pull the release rope! I yelled, "Hey! No!, It's against the law!"

As the hounds vaulted out and took off after the antelope, my rancher friend said, "It might be agin the law, but it ain't gonna hurt that antelope none!"

There was no roadside fence to slow either the hounds or our pickup truck. The antelope disappeared over a slight rise half a mile to the west, the dogs raising a huge cloud of dust in pursuit. We raced in the truck, jouncing and bouncing over the ruts, in chase of the chase. When we topped out on the slight rise, the pickup jolted to a stop. About a mile and a half ahead of us, the antelope pranced along slowly, his white rump patch flashing a sassy challenge. Half a mile on this side of him, the pack of five hounds walked slowly—turning their heads from side to side as if looking for a way out of their embarrassment. "Nope," said my friend, "those dogs can't catch everything that runs."

Chapter 22

The Effects of Control Measures

In the last eight chapters, we have described the methods used by man to kill coyotes. All of these, along with even more imaginative campaigns, have continuously been used against *Canis latrans* for many years. Surely, hasn't mankind almost eliminated the coyote?

No. Not so!

It is my informed guess that there are as many, and perhaps more, coyotes in the contiguous forty-eight states in 1983 as there ever have been! In 1983, the coyote occupies a larger range than he has ever occupied in his recorded history. The coyote has been responsible for driving about one half of America's sheepranchers out of business. Despite their best efforts, these ranchers have lost out to the coyote. No state can say that they have fewer coyotes now than in 1910!

Whenever there is a downward pressure exerted upon the coyote, the coyote species reacts by producing more pups per litter and more litters per year. Exactly how this biological reaction is triggered is one of the many mysteries we still do not understand about our wild neighbors.

The survivability of the coyote, as an individual and as a species, seems to increase during periods of greatest persecution. If steel traps are common over his range, the coyote becomes very expert at avoiding them. He will walk the tightrope between traps to reach his objective, and the catch per trap-day will go way, way down. It is easy to say that all of the stupid coyotes are quickly trapped off, accounting for the dwindling catch. It is also easy to say that we are simply applying the law of diminishing returns. "There are fewer coyotes to trap, hence we catch fewer." Logical, but not necessarily true. When trapping is intensified, there is some form of communication between coyotes—and the coyote redoubles his caution. It is much harder to trap coyotes after a few have been trapped in a given area. Coyotes are quick studiers and apt learners. They are also, (I believe), able to communicate the danger of steel traps among each other—hence lessening the danger.

When poisons are used, their effectiveness is greatest in the first few days. After that, the percentage of the available coyote population actually killed by poisons goes down rapidly. Within a few weeks a certain percentage of the remaining coyotes will not take a drop bait. When we use poisons in the vicinity of draw stations, such as a carcass of a horse or cow, the remaining coyotes quickly learn to give the draw station a wide berth.

Even with Compound 1080, which is by far the most effective of all control measures, we know of no warning factor—no way for the coyote to see, smell, or taste danger in the lethal bait station. Yet, even 1080 doesn't get the last unit of coyote population. There may be a certain percentage of coyotes which do not eat carrion—but I doubt it. Why then, do we fail to bag the last units of a population with Compound 1080? I have no answer.

Dog trainers will tell you that it is difficult to punish or reward a trainee at exactly the right moment. They will also tell you that it is senseless to punish an animal that has no idea what he did to merit the punishment. Canines have a relatively short memory, or so it seems. Training is based upon reinforcing good habits and punishment for bad habits—quickly, before the dog has a chance to forget the causative action on his part which brought him a swat with a rolled up newspaper, or a congratulatory pat.

Surely the same thing must be true of coyotes?

Wouldn't this make it almost impossible for the coyote to associate the pain and the dying caused by Compound 1080 with the delicious meal of carrion which the coyote ingested an hour earlier?

I have no answers.

But I do know that the coyote has been able to match our every move with a survival technique, to perfect his defenses and to go on producing larger litters of pups when they are needed to restock the coyote's niche in the environment. When coyote populations are not attacked, they reach an optimum number and seem to hold it—by producing fewer litters and fewer pups per litter. How? Again, I have no answers.

The only exception has been Compound 1080. As of this writing, that is not available for use in the war against coyotes.

Chapter 23

Guilty or Innocent?

Is the coyote a confirmed criminal when it comes to killing sheep? Do all coyotes kill sheep or are there only a few "killer types?" Is coyote predation on sheep flocks actually bad enough to cause extreme economic loss, or is it just a case of wild coyotes scavenging the carcasses of domestic sheep that have died of other causes?

Sheepmen have been telling us for many years that the coyote is a bad killer. But sheepmen are understandably prejudiced against the coyote. Perhaps it would be best to exclude all prejudicial evidence and only take down the facts reported by scientific research projects.

Let's start first with a few quotations from the master of science thesis written by one John R. Muñoz of Gonzaga University, as he worked in Montana, under direction of the University of Montana, to study coyote predation upon sheep on the Cook Ranch. These words were written in 1977, but neither coyotes nor sheep have changed much since then. I quote . . .

A combination of public pressure and the Cain Report influenced President Nixon, in 1972, to ban the use of poisons on federal lands and the Environmental Protection Agency to halt interstate shipment of chemical toxicants.

The initiatives were followed by complaints from stockmen, especially sheep ranchers. Where politicians had felt pressure

Spring lambs killed by coyotes for the fun of it and left uneaten.

to protect predators because they were deemed ecologically beneficial, sheepmen maintained that predators had little value in sheep grazing areas and should be controlled. In an effort to clarify an emotional and economic controversy, legislators authorized extensive funding for research in the field of livestock predation.

The Cook Ranch is located 22 miles south of Missoula just east of the Bitterroot River and west of the Lolo National Forest. The ranch consists of 6,064 acres owned by the Cooks, plus two thousand leased acres. It is divided into 28 pastures ranging from 3 to 816 acres. To the north and south the ranch borders on cattle and wheat ranches. Predators were hunted and trapped extensively prior to 1974, yet Cook reported approximately 12 percent (300 sheep) mortality to predators during 1973.

With that background information, we are ready to read along with Muñoz as he summarizes what he learned about the mortality of sheep on the Cook Ranch.

Total mortality, during both segments A and B, included deaths that occurred from the beginning of the lambing season until 14 March of the succeeding year. Field mortalities included only deaths recorded after sheep had been moved out of the lambing sheds. Total and field mortalities during both segments are recorded in Table 1. Field mortality for the entire herd were 19.8 and 21.7 percent of 2,664 and 3,712 sheep exposed to predation during segments A and B, respectively.

The percentage of predator kills, 16.3 during Segment B, compared to 16.9 for segment A, was again lower than the 18.3 percent predator losses reported by the State of Montana Department of Livestock (1974) for all of Montana from 1967 to 1969. Total mortality for lambs alone amounted to 10.9 percent of the 1,995 lambs born during 1975.

During segments A and B respectively, 355 of 397 (89.4 percent) and 486 of 617 (78.8 percent) lamb mortalities were attributed to predation."

How about the often-heard claim that coyotes kill only the lame, the halt, and the blind, that they actually may do some good by culling out the sick and diseased individuals from the herd? Muñoz continues:

Of the 602 sheep killed by coyotes during Segment B, health could be determined for 345 . . . the total percentage of healthy lambs killed was slightly less, whereas the percentage of lambs with abnormalities or severe disorders was slightly higher in Segment B than in A . . . Killing patterns in segments A and B indicated that coyotes were generally able to kill healthy sheep as easily as sick sheep.

Numbers of wounded, limping or sick sheep were recorded to determine whether or not they were later selected by coyotes. Results showed no significant selection for disabled sheep during either A or B.

Coyotes were responsible for 99.3 percent of predator kills found during Segment B, and 97.1 percent in segment A. Coyotes were responsible for 77.4 percent of all predator kills on the McKnight Ranch in New Mexico, 82 percent of predator losses on seven ranches in California, and 73 percent of all predator losses on selected ranches in Idaho.

One coyote was observed feeding on a ewe at 10:00 on 23 September 1975, and closer inspection, after the coyote left, revealed that the ewe was still alive, had a neck wound, and her abdomen was torn open.

But one cannot blame the coyote for killing sheep or eating them alive. After all, the animal is by nature a meat eater, and he wanted to eat to live, right?

De Lorenzo and Howard (1976) reported that 47.6 and 37.5 percent of the carcasses were not fed upon during 1974 and 1975 in New Mexico. This behavior is not completely understood, but Fox (1971) reported that the "prey killing response of a canid has a very high satiation level," a possible explanation for the phenomena of leaving carcasses intact and killing up to twelve sheep during a single night.

Another study of sheep losses to coyotes on the Cook Ranch was to have been completed by Kimber C. Brawley of the University of Utah, working on his master's degree requirements from the University of Montana in 1977, also. But his work was cut short, in the words of his master's thesis,

"My study began 15 March and ended 30 September 1976 when Cook sold the ranch because he felt he could not profitably raise sheep in the Bitterroot Valley due to coyote predation."

In a personal phone call to me in March of 1982, Bill Cook told me that coyotes had indeed forced him out of the sheep business in Montana and that he had moved to Arizona, buying a ranch there. When I suggested that this move might be jumping from the frying pan into the fire (as far as sheep ranching and coyotes were concerned) Cook laughed and replied, "No, I'm out of the sheep business entirely. Coyotes licked me; drove me out of that business."

Sometimes the honest actions of a rancher show more than many research studies might reveal.

How do coyotes go about killing sheep? Guy Connolly of the U.S. Fish and Wildlife Service, and Robert M. Timm, currently an extension wildlife specialist with the University of Nebraska, did some interesting work on this while at the University of California at Davis.

Summary points taken from their report, as reprinted in the *National Wool Grower* January, 1980, are as follows:

They put coyotes with no previous sheep killing experience in pens with sheep, and although the coyotes were mostly pen-raised, they quickly proved themselves capable of killing sheep. Sheep which turned and ran from the coyotes were more often chosen as victims, and the coyotes chose lambs over ewes when given the chance. The *modus operandi* of the killing was: The coyote generally ran alongside the fleeing sheep, bit it in the throat area behind the ear, and then braced its feet to stop the sheep from running. As soon as the sheep is brought to a stop, the coyote shifts its tooth-hold to secure a firm grip in the larynx region, where it holds on—till the sheep suffocates, or at least falls down. To quote "The time from onset of attack to the death of the sheep, or beginning of feeding, whichever came first, averaged thirteen minutes." And another quote, "As soon as the sheep stopped struggling, the coyote began feeding."

How did Connolly and Timm learn these facts about coyotes methods of killing sheep? In their words,

In our tests, one to four coyotes were released into a .4 acre pen with one to six sheep, usually for two to five hours. The coyotes killed one or more sheep in 22 of the 46 tests. For the tests in which a fatal attack occurred, the time from release of coyotes to onset of attack varied from 1 to 154 minutes. Of the coyotes tested individually with single lambs, the dominant animals (two year old males and the females paired with them) attacked most frequently. Yearling males attacked less frequently, and the two unpaired females did not attack sheep.

But those coyotes were forced to kill, their advocates might say. They were starved to it. In fact, they had to kill to live. But what really happens under usual ranch conditions? Well, we've already seen the history of the Cook Ranch in Montana—where coyotes killed so many sheep that the owner was forced to sell the ranch and get out of the sheep business. But that's up north; what would happen in a warmer clime, where lots of rodent food was available to the hungry coyote?

During the annual Sheep and Goat Raisers Convention in 1979, Texas ranchers were asked to volunteer their flocks for a test of the toxic collar, a device aimed at killing only coyotes which killed sheep. The collar is punctured by the coyote in his killing attempt and the coyote gets a lethal dose of the poison.

Charles Howard volunteered his Angora goat ranching operation located near Meridian, Texas, which is south and slightly west of Fort Worth. Mr. Howard said that he had been raising goats since 1965, but in April of 1979 he lost so many goats that it was necessary to gather and pen his goats every night to stop the predation. When his goats roamed the pastures only by day, the coyotes began killing by day. Finally, he was down to a system of penning at night and trying to feed 800 goats in a 24 acre pasture in the day time. This crowding brought on parasitism and sickness to the Angora flock.

Wildlife specialist Dale A. Wade of the Texas A & M Extension Service and Guy Connolly of the U.S. Fish and Wildlife Denver Research Center staff, recorded the statistics of the Howard Angora operation as follows: "Close confinement of goats caused parasite infestations and reduced thriftiness. Nearly all kids born in 1979 were lost, some to coyotes, some to disease, some simply disappeared. Of the normal kid crop of 240 kids, only 27 kids survived—which means that predators killed, directly or indirectly, some 213 kids."

Why did coyotes hit this flock of Angora goats so hard? It wasn't because they were starved into it, or forced to kill goats. There was an abundance of their natural prey—wild rodents, rabbits, and mice on the area. Whitetailed deer were also abundant in the area. No, the coyotes did not kill because of any scarcity of natural prey. They killed because they liked to kill, because the goats were easily caught and easily killed.

Toxic collars helped the Howard goat operation stay in business. We will have a more detailed discussion of the toxic collar later.

Perhaps we ought to face the facts. Coyotes kill sheep and goats because they like to kill sheep and goats. We have seen that the presence or absence of a large supply of coyote food in the form of rodents does not guarantee that the coyote will eat hits "natural food" and leave sheep and goats alone.

The presence of a large number of rodents does guarantee that the coyote will stay in the area and be able to kill sheep and goats when a meal of mutton strikes his fancy.

Chapter 24

Alternative Control Methods

Spurred on by humanitarian considerations and a natural aversion to killing an animal which is only "doing its thing," people have long sought alternative methods of stopping the economic loss caused by coyotes without killing coyotes. Other proposals decree death for the offending coyote—the actual animal which is killing sheep, or stealing turkeys—but not of other coyotes who may never have killed a domestic animal in their life. Why kill the innocent coyotes? Wouldn't it be better to take only those which are known to be killers and leave the valuable mouser alone?

This is obviously a worthy goal. Some of the proposed alternative methods are: repellents that make the sheep smell bad enough so that the coyotes won't be attracted to them; the extension trapper system, which endeavors to kill only "guilty" coyotes; reproduction inhibitors to reduce the number of coyotes, not by killing them, but by preventing their birth; keeping llamas, donkeys, or sheep dogs, to protect flocks from marauding coyotes; employing sheepherders—dedicated men who live with the sheep and protect them; changing the system of sheep culture to keep the animals tightly herded and in pens at night where they can be more easily protected from predators; toxic collars to kill the coyote that attempts to cut the throat of the sheep; and guard dogs and exploders to keep coyotes at bay. Obviously, there are many other suggested alternatives—some of them humorous, some of them partially effective, all of them well meant.

Why not spray the sheep with a repellent? This would make the sheep smell bad, and repel the coyote, as it were. This was tried in one of the big sheep-raising states in the west. The coyotes stayed away; the sheep were not killed. There was a side effect which no one had anticipated. It seems that the male sheep—the ram—finds the receptive female sheep—the ewe—by means of smell. When oestreus hits the ewe, her body puts out a chemical that the educated nose of the ram detects. The ram then goes to that particular ewe, which is receptive to his services, and breeds her. If he doesn't breed the ewe, and her oestreus passes without her being bred, there will be no lamb, of course, next spring.

The repellent, which made the sheep smell bad to the coyote, also made the ewe smell bad to the ram. He didn't smell the particular odor which tells him which ewe is receptive. He didn't breed the ewe and there were no lambs in the spring.

Oh, well, back to the old drawing board!

Other repellent chemicals have been tried, of course, and some of them have had some beneficial effect in reducing sheep mortality from coyotes. But the effects have been short lived, and it is necessary to keep applying the chemical—at one week intervals, to ensure their effectiveness. This becomes economically ineffective.

Other candidate chemicals have worked, until the coyote learned that the same juicy, tender lamb was behind the odor. Then the adaptable coyote quickly adapted and returned to dining on leg of lamb—regardless of the repellent odor.

The Extension Trapper System

An alternative system which has been used for years is the extension trapper system. Missouri was the first state to try this system in coyote control. We will take a good long look at this alternative in this chapter. Remember, though, Missouri is not really within the original range of the coyote, but rather lies east of that known range. We also want to point out the background against which the drama of the extension trapper system is being played out.

Missouri paid a thirty dollar bounty on coyotes in 1953 but the bounty law was repealed a few years later. Several counties went broke paying the bounty without state help, especially along the Kansas border, where they probably were buying Kansas coyotes. The legislature then quietly quit appropriating money to pay for bounties. In 1982, a few counties are still paying bounties, but the bounty program is no longer large enough to be statistically significant.

Before we go into the description of the Missouri extension trapper program, we should take a good look at the Missouri residents' attitude toward coyotes. In 1953, my good friend Jim Keefe wrote a piece about coyotes for the *Missouri Conservationist* magazine. Jim is now the chief information officer for Missouri's Department of Conservation—known as one of the most progressive in the nation. We believe the piece to be a good presentation of the Missouri coyote. It was correct in 1953. It is still an accurate portrayal thirty years later. With permission of Jim Keefe, and of the Missouri Department of Conservation, we will present the February 1953 article entitled *"Outcast in Grey"* in its entirety. To understand how Missouri residents have felt about the coyote, turn to Appendix I at the end of this book.

The extention trapper program began in 1945 with the employment of two former Fish and Wildlife Service trappers. In 1947, Missouri took over full supervision of the program. Shortly after that, they took over all funding of the program. How did this program differ from the cooperatively funded federal trapper program? Many parts of the program were the same, but there was a fundamental difference. In the extension program, the emphasis was on having the professional government trapper train the farmer, rather than do the actual trapping himself.

The three extension trappers who were employed around about 1980 did both kinds of work. They responded directly to serious damage complaints and did some coyote removal themselves. In addition, they scheduled control demonstrations, in response to popular request, and showed the interested onlookers how to trap coyotes and foxes (and other mammalian nuisances).

An economist would probably say that there is no difference between the federal-state cooperative program which employed full time professionals to do the actual trapping, and the state extension program which taught the individual to do his own trapping. In the federal cooperative program, the people pay the freight, through their taxes and self-imposed contributions to the program. In the state extension program, the people still pay the costs of the program—partly through their taxes (of one sort or another), and partly through their own self-imposed contributions of time and money—time to do the work (which is done by a full time employee in the federal program) and money to buy their own traps and other equipment.

The direct cost—the evident cost—of the state program is much less than the federal cost. When all costs are assessed to the program, the actual cost of removing one predator is probably very nearly the same in each program.

For Missouri, with its small farm flock system of sheep production, the extension trapper system has definite advantages. The landowner/operator can do his own predator control work in his small area in his "spare time." In comparison, the large western sheepman, running as many as 10,000 sheep on a range of as much as fifty sections of land, has no chance of doing this work in his "spare time."

Obviously, the full time professional will attain a greater degree of skill in using control methods than will the part time farmer's son (or farmer) who learns how from the extension trapper instructor. But the greater expertise is probably not needed on the small flock.

The most effective tools of the full time professional are the coyote-getter and the poison known as 1080. These tools can only be used in areas of low human and domestic animal density. Take away these two tools, and the federal trapper is reduced to the same tools that his less skillful (less schooled) part time counterpart uses under the extension trapper program. Obviously, coyote-getters and 1080 would wreak havoc with farm dogs in the more densely populated Missouri farm country.

There will always be an argument about the effectiveness of the extension trapper system. Its proponents point to a great reduction in number of complaints received, citing this as evidence that the "trained" landowner is now doing his own work. Opponents shrug and say "No use putting in a complaint. You don't get any real help, anyway. Just another slide show and movie about how to set traps." Those in favor of the program point to a great reduction in governmental funds appropriated for coyote control work. The antis say, "Sure, now we spend our own time and money, in an amateur way, to do the same thing. Is that cost-effective?"

There will never be full agreement, naturally.

I'd like to add my two cents worth, if I may. I think the extension trapper system works very well in Missouri, and will work in other densely populated states with small flocks to protect. I think the government trapper works far better on large flocks of sheep and/or goats, and works best in the states with wide open spaces and low human density.

The extension trapper system? For Missouri, yessir! For Texas west of the Pecos, "No way!"

But that's only one man's opinion.

Planned Parenthood for Coyotes

In the fall of 1962, I was promoted from principal assistant in the Texas District to become the regional information officer for an eight state region of the U.S. Fish and Wildlife Service. This was a wonderful break for me, as it allowed me to roam through the "coyote-fighting" states of Arizona, Wyoming, Kansas, and Texas, and all points in between. I wrote a news release on April 12, 1964. I'd like to quote it in its entirety:

Birth Control Reaches the Western Range

For the past few years, there has been a population explosion on the western range—a steady increase in the numbers of coyotes, the number one animal enemy of the stockman. At the same time, more humans use the western range. Because there are so many rockhounds, hunters, fishermen, photographers, campers, hikers, or just plain visitors using new-found leisure hours on the federal lands of the west, it is becoming increasingly difficult for the Bureau of Sport Fisheries and Wildlife's Branch of Predator and Rodent Control to control the numbers of coyotes. Cyanide getters cannot safely be used where children play, nor can poisons selective to the canine family by employed where the tourists's pet dog will roam. The coyote doesn't mind the increase in people, for Don Coyote is very adaptable, but the increase in public use hampers the control activities of the predator control men. With curtailed predator control, the sheepmen suffer greater losses, the mohair goat raiser finds it almost impossible to operate at a profit, and the poultryman reports greater losses. In Texas and Oklahoma, coyotes cause heavy losses among newborn calves.

Something has to be done to stop the population explosion of coyotes without endangering the vacation seekers invading the scenic wonderlands of the West.

At the end of the first phase of experimentation, evidence is mounting that the Bureau's Branch of Wildlife Research has come up with the answer to the problem. Birth control—for coyotes only, of course.

Planned parenthood for predators is fast becoming a reality. Don Balser, a research scientist with the Bureau's Control Methods Research Section, operates out of the Wildlife Research Center in Denver, Colorado, testing the results of feeding stilbestrol to coyotes during the breeding season. Initial results have been good. The coyote that eats a bait treated with this reproduction inhibiting chemical simply does not become pregnant. If embryo implantation has taken place when the stilbestrol is ingested, the embryos are resorbed by the female and she does not give birth. The coyote doesn't know that any change has taken place, but when the annual crop of pups is prevented from being born, the population of coyotes in the treated area drops sharply.

It seems that research has come up with a tool in coyote control which comes near to pleasing everyone. Groups of people who objected to other control methods in the belief that they were cruel or caused suffering to the animal can find no objection to the reproduction inhibitor which causes no pain, no suffering—no change at all—except that no pups are born that spring.

Those that feared coyote control programs because of alleged harmful effects on other species can now rest easier. The breeding season of coyotes coincides with the breeding season of very few other mammals; hence, only the coyote is affected.

Dog lovers who feared poisons, traps, and cyanide getters because they feared for Old Rover's safety, can relax when the method of control is the reproduction inhibitor. If a dog takes one of the stilbestrol baits, the only result is that it cannot be bred that particular season. As coyotes come into season only once a year—and dogs more often—there can be no loss to the dog lover.

The sheepman who feared the coyote because it killed hapless newborn lambs in the spring when it had a den full of pups to feed, can breathe easier. Relieved of the necessity of foraging for a litter of hungry pups, the adult coyote does not need to kill as often and is more apt to content itself with natural foods—sparing the sheep.

In 1963, a team of men operating under Mr. Balser's direction, placed the reproduction inhibiting baits on a 720 square mile area in southeastern New Mexico. Government trappers kept track of the number of denning females taken and performed autopsies on all females taken in normal control operations. Results were very encouraging, so this year the testing area is being enlarged. At the present time, reproduction inhibiting baits are being exposed on the Mountain Home desert in Idaho, and on 150 townships in southern New Mexico. These areas were selected either because they had a high coyote population or because they were areas that have been traditional trouble spots, with heavy losses to marauding coyotes. After the drug has had time to take effect, Mr. Balser's men will take every coyote they can to examine reproductive tracts and to determine whether or not the Planned Parenthood Program has succeeded or failed.

Research scientist Balser is careful to point out that this program is definitely still in the research stage, but livestock interests all over the West are watching eagerly for the results of the larger tests this spring. If initial results of 1963 are confirmed by the more extensive tests of 1964, then we can say that research has solved still another knotty problem of wildlife management. Maybe soon we can adjust the number of coyotes to suit the needs of the land—and the landowners—without endangering other species of wildlife or domestic animals. Maybe Planned Parenthood for Coyotes is the answer!

Naturally, there is a story behind that news release. Early in 1960, the Denver Research Center (DRC) began to experiment with the idea of reproduction inhibitors for coyotes. The goal was simple and ideal. It would be so much nicer for all concerned if, instead of having to kill coyotes, the coyotes simply were never born at all.

A careful scientist, Balser wanted to be sure of what he was doing when the field experiment started; so he ran controlled tests on female coyotes in pens at the (DRC). He had a long list of candidate drugs, but was forced to discard many of them. The progestational compounds required daily dosages (what if the wild females missed her Pill?) and when the dosage was stopped, oestreus occurred at once and the female was ready to get pregnant. He narrowed the field down to the synthetic estrogens simply because they were effective for a long period of time after being swallowed, and because they negatively affected reproduction much earlier in the reproduction cycle.

After Balser's cage tests in 1961 and 1962, his candidate chemicals were narrowed down to the chemical stilbestrol.

When it came time to do the field testing, Don selected five areas in New Mexico, some with many coyotes, some with few. Knowing that the coyote has shown evidence of being density-affected in reproduction (when there are many breeding females, the average litter will be small; when there are few breeding females, the average litter will be large), Don wanted to test the control method in all varying conditions. Another test area was selected in the Mountain Home desert area of Idaho. In the Idaho area, the reproduction inhibitor was administered much earlier in the season, to see if it could get results over the long period of oestreus. It didn't work.

After lots of experimenting, Balser and his helpers perfected a bait formula that combined a small amount of beeswax with a large vat of animal fat—lard—as a carrier for the stilbestrol. When maintained at the correct temperature, the mixture would flow through a nozzle so the operator filled tiny paper cups with the dose. Cooled, the carrier solidified quickly, and made an easily-handled but quite tough bait.

Tests on caged animals showed that this mixture would be readily accepted by coyotes, which have very broad appetites. Laboratory tests run by independent laboratories showed that each dose contained approximately one hundred milligrams of stilbestrol, enough to product the desired results. Perhaps we should say, the desired "lack" of results.

Airplanes were used to drop some 55,500 baits in the New Mexico test area, and ground crews placed another 17,500 baits in areas that coyotes used quite heavily. The scene was set for the big experiment.

Baits were placed during the second week in March. At that time, coyote breeding should have been just past its peak. Because the stilbestrol works best when ingested during the first fifteen days of prenancy, the drop time was statistically calculated to interrupt reproduction for the maximum number of coyote females. When pregnancy has proceeded past the 45th day, the stilbestrol has no effect. In Mountain Home, Idaho, the compound was exposed for coyotes during the last week of January, much before the peak of the reproduction season.

Reproductive tracts were collected from females taken in other areas of New Mexico and Idaho, starting in early April when all female coyotes had either whelped or would be carrying well developed embryos. This was done to establish the "normal" reproductive success for each area. The results from the treated areas could be compared with those control areas.

Examination of the reproductive tracts in the Fort Bliss area of New Mexico showed that 80 percent of the adult females had NOT reproduced. In the Malaga area of New Mexico, 16 of 33 mature females were not successful in giving birth. In Idaho, the early placement of baits had been aimed at blocking ovulation. This test failed to show the desired results. In the treated area, reproduction was 89 percent successful; in the untreated area it was 100 percent successful.

The stage was set for painless, peaceful control of coyote numbers without traps, getters, poisons, dogs, airplanes, snares, and den hunting. Farm and ranch dogs, wild-ranging hounds, and the family pet that wandered away from the picnic ground would not be endangered.

It seemed that stilbestrol—Planned Parenthood for coyotes—was the answer to a biologist's prayer.

Then what happened?

After several more years of testing, the stilbestrol program was stopped.

Why?

It would be most accurate to say that the program was stopped because it simply did not work. It turned out to be impossible to perfect delivery techniques that would get the stilbestrol into a high enough percentage of the breeding age female coyotes to *materially* affect the number of pregnancies over a large area.

Wait a minute! We saw the good results of the first tests. It worked!

The results were not significant, sayeth the computer. The slight drop we noticed after the New Mexico tests was a natural abberation, which would have occurred without the stilbestrol. Sound hard to believe?

After the tremendous effort of baiting a large area with stilbestrol desserts, research scientists killed many female coyotes to check their pregnancy record written in their reproductive organs. They found reproductive success was almost the same in the treated areas as it was in the untreated control area nearby.

The research scientists felt Planned Parenthood for coyotes was no longer an attainable goal—at least not with any of the chemicals available then. Sam Linhart, of the DRC, feels that we can write this method off. Others disagree. The stakes are high; and many people would be very happy if successful reproductive inhibitors could be delivered. The U.S. Department of Agriculture is also at work on the problem—not working with delivery systems, but only trying to find the correct chemical. Dr. Jeffrey Green is engaged in this work at the Sheep Experiment Station, Dubois, Idaho, and perhaps the Department of Agriculture will succeed where the U.S. Fish and Wildlife Service did not succeed.

In the eyes of the coyote control researchers at the DRC, we can add this planned parenthood to the long and growing list of things man has tried to use against coyotes—and found ineffective. Steel traps, leg snares, strychnine, thallium sulphate, cyanide getters, aerial hunting, sight-running hounds, predator calls—the list grows ever longer and the coyote grows ever smarter to avoid these dangers.

In all the recorded history of man-versus-coyote, the only weapon developed by man which the coyote seems unable to cope with and has reduced coyote populations below a threatening level is Compound 1080, sodium monoflouroacetate. True, 1080 has never proved to be an "eradicator," but few want to exterminate the coyote. Although far more species specific than any other control method used to date, Compound 1080 does pose some definite hazards, and it produces a death which is less than lovely to witness.

Stilbestrol? It looked so good, and it would have been so nice to reduce coyote numbers by simply causing them "not to be born."

Too bad it didn't work out.

It is worth mentioning that the Department of Agriculture seems less anxious to write off reproduction inhibitors than is the Department of the Interior. John N. Stellflug, Norman L. Gates, and Charles W. Leathers collaborated in a report of "Anti-testicular Activity of DL-6-(N-2-Pipecolinomethyl)-5 Hydroxy-Indane-Maleate (PMHI) in Coyotes, *(Canis latrans)*." I wouldn't be surprised if that title scares you off. It means that they tested a chemical that was supposed to cause infertility in male coyotes. These were caged animal tests, and they were successful. The last sentence of the abstract of their report says, "We conclude that PMHI may cause infertility in the male coyote from 15 to at least 82 days after treatment without apparent damage to vital organs."

Stellflug, Gates, and R. Garth Sasser collaborated on a report presented to the Eighth Vertebrate Pest Control Conference, 1978, on the research the Department of Agriculture has done in light of the earlier work done by the U.S. Fish and Wildlife Service. The Fish and Wildlife Service seems to have surrendered this field of study to the agriculture people. The Stellflug report is a good source of information about the various classes of chemicals that still offer hope for development of an effective reproduction inhibitor. Two quotations from this report are worth our study now:

> During the last ten years, interest in reproductive inhibitors for the male has increased. Most of this work has been directed toward rodent population control. The results of this research have provided us with several antifertility compounds that may be worth evaluating for effectiveness in coyotes.

And the conclusion of the report says,

> Research on reproductive inhibitors for coyote control is still in a stage of infancy. Eventual success in developing practical, effective, acceptable methods of coyote population control by anti-fertility methods will require intensive interdisciplinary effort. More basic knowledge of the reproductive physiology is most urgently needed and may lead to valuable insight as to where our major emphasis for control should be placed. Concurrently, more research is required on the most promising compounds. In the female, several prostaglandin analogues and 14ng acting estrogenic compounds should be considered. In the male, boron, low doses of PMHI, TEM and a combination of busulfan and MMS appears most promising to date. *The needs and challenges are great.* [Emphasis supplied by CLC.]

Perhaps continuing research will come up with a method of planned parenthood for coyotes that works. If it is realized, we can honestly say that we have the ability to substitute coyote management for coyote control, our euphemism for coyote killing.

Toxic Collars

Why not take advantage of the fact that coyotes usually kill sheep by biting the throat? Why not protect that part of the anatomy with a collar containing a toxic material? If the coyote bites through the collar, he gets a lethal dose of the poison and dies. This would be poetic justice that the killer kills himself by attacking the collared victim.

Roy McBride tried this idea out in west Texas, putting lethal 1080 collars on sheep exposed to coyotes. In most cases of sheep mortality, the coyote obligingly killed by the neck and got a dose from the lethal collar. It worked, and justice was served.

After Roy came up with the idea in 1974, the Denver Wildlife Research Center gave the toxic collar top priority in their control methods research. Branching out a little, they tested various lethal agents in the toxic collar—sodium cyanide in 1975, diphacinone in 1976, Compound 1080 from 1978 through 1981, and methomyl in 1981. As of late 1981, the research people had come to the conclusion that 1080 was the safest and most effective poison available and they put in an application for EPA registration of 1080 in livestock collars. As of this writing that application still has not been resolved.

In most cases, toxic collars are the "radical surgery" method of treating a bad case of coyote predation. Obviously, the lamb is a sacrificial lamb. The collar does not protect it from death, but merely exacts swift retribution on the killer. Reporting on the use of the collars in field tests, Guy Connolly told to the Fifth Great Plains Wildlife Damage Control Workshop in Lincoln, Nebraska in October of 1981, that 28 field tests had been carried out in Alberta, Texas, Idaho, and Montana. In 17 of these tests, Connolly reported, predation stopped or declined following short-term (under 30 days) or long term use of collars. The other 11 tests did not produce evidence of collar effectiveness, primarily because coyotes did not attack collared livestock.

The toxic collar offers the advantage of not raising the hackles of those who fear injury to non-target species. After all, any animal that bites the neck of a sheep has got it coming to him, right? It is an expensive method of killing a coyote—back in 1981 the toxic collar cost more than sixteen bucks each, to say nothing of the expense of catching the sheep and hand-collaring them. Also, some coyotes kill by different methods than by biting the neck. I remember examining 22 sheep killed in one pasture by

166

coyotes. Every single one of them had been killed by a puncture bite to the head. These were small lambs. The coyote—or coyotes—involved enjoyed picking them up by a bite to the skull, giving one quick lethal bite, and dropping one to race on to the next. None of the 22 sheep had been eaten. Connolly reported that 70 percent of all sheep attacks (in their studies) resulted in the puncture of the collar, however.

Following up on the idea of getting a lethal chemical into the coyote that kills a sheep, some experimentation has been carried on in the field of placing a scented, coyote-attractive, package of some kind on the sheep. The hope is that the coyote will chew it after he kills the sheep, thus poisoning himself. Small packets of 1080 have been fastened to the ear in a scented package. The killer coyote smells the scented package and chews it off of the sheep he has killed. This method shows some promise and is being examined. It is a logical outgrowth of the "trap-tabs" that were placed on steel leghold traps.

All of these methods have the great advantage of being directed solely toward the coyote which is doing the killing. If a coyote is not killing sheep, it has nothing to fear from the toxic collar.

Developing an Aversion to Mutton

Considerable experimental work has been done with a chemical known as lithium chloride. The chemical causes severe nausea and other uncomfortable symptoms in coyotes that ingest the lithium chloride bait material. By putting out sheep carcasses treated with lithium chloride, it was hoped that the coyote would develop an aversion to sheep flesh—because it made the coyote sick.

Some of the more optimistic proponents of this method of reducing economic losses caused by coyotes even claimed that the lactating female would transmit the aversion to her pups. However, it was found that the amount of lithium chloride in Momma Coyote's milk was about one twentieth of what was required to develop the aversion in the young.

It seems that the coyotes being studied didn't like the lithium chloride, but were smart enough to know that it was the chemical that didn't taste good and made them sick, not the tasty young lamb, or the stringy old mutton for that matter. In some tests, coyotes were offered lithium chloride treated jackrabbit carcasses. After a short period of time the coyotes stopped eating the treated jackrabbit carcasses, but continued to kill and eat fresh jackrabbit. Evidently the coyote is too intelligent to be fooled by such aversion developing chemicals. Kind of reminds me of the bumper sticker which says, "Eat Lamb—50,000 coyotes can't be wrong!" The coyote knows what it wants to eat, regardless of behavior modification conditioning to the contrary.

Llamas, Donkeys, and Dogs

Other than man himself, is it possible to enlist the help of another mammal to protect the sheep against the coyote? We had heard of a case where llamas, the South American mammal, had been pastured with the sheep and had done yeoman duty in protecting the sheep from the coyote. This was on the Lye Ranch, near Pavillion, Wyoming, in the heart of coyote country. In reply to our letter, Mrs. Lye replied as follows:

Pavillion, Wyoming 82523
March 9, 1982

Mr. Cadieux,

 The University of Wyoming and our farm are the only places that have a llama used to protect sheep. This is still in the experimental stage but we do feel we have some results.

 The FENCE POST, an agricultural paper, had an article on the University of Wyoming llamas—they have two llamas in a pasture with lambs and have put in two coyotes with them. The article was called "A Waiting Game." I have not heard the results yet but we do not expect a complete protection since we did lose some lambs last year even though we did have our llama with the sheep. We think we had less killed, however.

 We live four miles west of Pavillion or 1½ miles north of Morton. We have recently put our farm up for sale. We will not leave the land but keep 20 acres and our registered sheep. We love the farm and our sheep so we have tried the llama as a last resort. We had eleven coyotes killed on our place in one month last fall. We have our biggest loss June through October when the coyote pelts are not good so trappers aren't interested in them. If you want more information please let us know.

 I hope the story you write about the coyotes gives a true story of them. They will be the last survivors on earth—too cunning for man.

Sincerely,

(sgd) Betty L. Lye

Llamas used as guardians for sheep against coyote predation, on the ranch of John and Betty Lye, Pavillion, Wyoming.

The llama is obviously too big an animal to be easily pulled down by coyotes, and it displays an aggressive behavior in the face of any threat to the sheep. It is not known, yet, whether two llamas would be better at protecting the sheep than one, or no good at all. When the llama is alone, it stays with the sheep and guards them from an approaching coyote. If there are two llamas, some animal behaviorists feel that they would stay by themselves, leaving the sheep at the mercy of a coyote.

Why does the llama take it upon itself to fight for the coyote? No one has a good answer to that question as of yet, so we will have to wait until more experience is gained with the guard llama system.

Mr. William J. Pursell of the Triple P Ranch in Indiana tells me that he has successfully used a donkey with foal to guard his sheep in a small flock. In his words, "My success rate has been very good. In our operation we have 35 ewes with one jenny and foal on 20 acre pasture. Some area farmers have run larger pastures with success. Since 1976, no sheep have been lost to predators during the time they were with donkeys. My only experience with donkeys shows that jennys with foal are the most effective. In my county, coyotes and large dogs are increasing rapidly. To date no loss has occurred where donkeys were present. Strikes have been commonplace where there were no donkeys. Our experience shows that jacks were undesirable; in one case, the jack killed sheep." More evidence will have to come in before we can decide whether or not the donkey-protector system has any validity. Mr. Pursell says that he feels that one donkey, or donkey with foal, provides the best protection for his small band of sheep. He feels that a larger grouping, with more than two donkeys, would probably result in the donkeys bunching together and not protecting the sheep. In any event, it would seem to have little application to the sheep ranching method, where thousands of sheep are run in one flock.

Many years ago, I had the opportunity to become acquainted with the very best system of protecting sheep from coyotes. The best method is to have a full time Basque sheepherder, complete with sheep wagon and two good sheepdogs, to spend all of his time with the sheep.

There is something about the Basque personality, a grand-scale patience, a love of doing a good job in the out-of-doors, that suited the occupation of sturdy Catalan-speaking men I met in the early 1960s in Wyoming's sheep country. They drove a team of two horses, both of which were broke to ride, that pulled their sheep wagon into the range land in the spring. In most cases the herders brought their sheep out in the fall. During a five or even six months period they lived with the sheep, guarding them with their lives. The rancher who employed the herders brought groceries to them in his pickup once a month. In many cases, they did not see another human being for months at a time. The herders didn't understand my Spanish, and I couldn't even pick up a word of Catalan, so we did no communicating.

The rancher told me that he had contracted for the man's services, guaranteeing his passage by tramp steamer, over and back, in return for one year's work. That was the perfect system. I say "It was," because it is no longer possible to find Basques that will do that terribly lonely job for pay low enough to make it economic. Those days are long gone.

We have not discussed the alternative of herding sheep by day and penning them securely at night. It works, of course, but it is very expensive. We feel that it is not cost effective when we are talking about large sheep operations.

I remember a conversation I had with a Wyoming sheep man who was going out of business because of coyote depredations. I told him about how sheep are penned in small flock operations farther east. He told me how much it cost him to hire that kind of help, to build that kind of fences, and argued that it was economically unsound. "I simply cannot compete here any

170

more," was his mournful conclusion.

"What would it take to make you competitive?" I asked.

"I guess the only thing would be turn loose some coyotes in New Zealand and Australia!" he replied.

Chapter 25

How Many Kinds of Coyotes?

Mammalogists, like other scientists in the field of biology or zoology, desire to name a sub-species after themselves, or at least to get credit "in the literature" for naming a new sub-species. This leads to the automatic creation of a group of taxonomists known as "splitters" who find a new species every time they find a slight difference in pelage color or a slightly smaller tooth measurement in a specimen.

Then there is another school of thought, which I would belong to, if I were qualified enough to call myself a taxonomist—the school known as "lumpers." They refuse to recognize sub-speciation unless the differences are so great that it would be intellectually clumsy to lump them under the same name.

Taxonomists use color of coat, size of animal, skull shape, wide or narrow spreading zygomata, measurements between maxillae, and a hundred other measurements as determining factors in their arguments for and against sub-species status. But the extent of individual variation among pups in the same litter is great at times, and color of fur is a very fickle determinant. We can cite hundreds of examples of other birds and animals whose fur or feathers change color with changes in diet. The flamingo is a wonderful example of this color shift with diet.

When one coyote sub-species is described as having a grayish umber pelt with slightly ochreous tints on the forelegs, and another is described as having a reddish gray pelt with rufous tints to the foreparts—one gets to wondering. The individual variations exceed those variations the splitters look for between sub-species.

Perhaps the most authoritative listing of coyote subspecies ever compiled was that of Hartly H. T. Jackson, a biologist with the U.S. Fish and Wildlife Service, who contributed the section, "Classification of the Races of the Coyote" to Stanley P. Young's 1951 book on the coyote. Thirty some years ago, Jackson felt that there was reason to assign sub-species status to nineteen different races of coyotes, based on what he called substantial differences between the races. The nineteen sub-species in his classification were roughly described as:

(1) *Canis latrans latrans,* found from the southern half of Saskatchewan and the southeastern corner of Alberta, in Canada, southward to eastern Colorado and the northern tip of the Texas Panhandle and the western half of Oklahoma. In his description of the subspecies, Jackson used the following terminology: "Compared with *C.l. lestes,* the subspecies *latrans* averages slightly smaller, much paler in general color tone, the muzzle, ears, and leg color being near pinkish buff to pinkish cinnamon or cinnamon as contrasted with near cinnamon to sayal brown or darker (almost snuff brown) of *lestes:* skull slightly smaller than that of *lestes,* usually with somewhat weaker dentition."

I believe that descriptive terms must be able to stand by themselves to point up differences; it is not enough to be "somewhat" paler. Nor can I hope to distinguish between pinkish cinnamon and buff cinnamon. As for the color description of "snuff brown," I am tempted to ask if the snuff was fresh or stale, used or pristine in the can. It is not my intent or purpose to poke fun at the overly cautious language of the species descriptions, for Jackson did a remarkably good job, wrote very complete descriptions, and tried his level best to be conscientious. However, there is no type specimen in existence of the *latrans latrans* coyote as of the time that Jackson did his writing. He completes his description of the *Canis latrans latrans* animals with the words, "can generally be recognized as the palest and grayest of the coyotes."

(2) Intergradation between *C.l. latrans* and *C.l. incolatus* is common along the line dividing their territories. *Incolatus* is found from middle of Alberta and Saskatchewan, northward to take in (now) all of Alaska. There are marked cranial measurement differences between this sub-species and others, but other charac-

teristics are remarkably constant through its range. The sub-species probably moved steadily northward in extending its range, and that all of the Alaskan coyotes seem to have come from the same parent stock. But I have a question. Where did they come from, if their range overlaps only that of the numerous *C.l. latrans,* the relatively rare *C.l. thamnos* or Great Lakes Coyote, and the *C.l.lestes* of the intermountain west? It is my belief that most of these northward voyaging coyotes came from *latrans,* the typical (if such a thing can be said) coyote of the center of the original range, the Great Plains. If my guess is right, it seems strange that they developed strikingly different cranial measurements in the few short decades between the appearance of the first coyotes in Alaska and the time of Jackson's compilation. Jackson theorized that the coyote had always been resident in Alaska, and merely increased in population density, rather than spreading its range. However, early writers of Alaska stress the existence of the true wolf, but called the smaller coyote either rare or non-existent.

(3) *Canis latrans thamnos,* the true coyote of the northern Great Lakes region, characterized by bigger, more fearsome teeth than the *latrans* coyote. *C.l. thamnos* was rarely seen when the timber wolf ruled the roost in the more heavily forested areas of the northern United States. From northern Missouri through Iowa and Minnesota, northward to northern Saskatchewan and even on into the Northwest Territories, it was found as far east as western New York State.

(4) *Canis latrans frustror,* is the name given to the "southeast" coyote of the United States. It is the largest of all the sub-species, which is logical because both its type locality and assumed range nearly borders the area of greatest known concentration of the red wolf, the so-called *Canis niger.* It would be a good guess that the large size of *frustror* is a result of interbreeding with the red wolf, which became rarer and rarer during the first half of the 1900s. In the descriptions of *frustror* one finds many words like rufous, richly colored, rich fulvous, to describe the coloration . . . which backs up the red wolf theory. Found from eastern Kansas, Okla-homa, and Texas south of the Missouri river in that state, and on into northwestern Arkansas. Jackson felt that there might be possible hybridization between this coyote and the red wolf, but not "intergradation." To my simple mind, it would seem that hybridization is the causative action which produces inter-gradation, but perhaps that is too simplistic.

175

(5) *Canis latrans texensis,* is found across all of eastern New Mexico and all of Texas except the eastern one-third. The type locality for this sub-species is 45 miles southwest of Corpus Christi, at Santa Gertrudis, Kleberg County, Texas—which is slightly south and west of good red wolf habitat. *C.l. texensis* is listed as a medium-sized coyote. Merriam and Bailey and other pioneers thought that *mearnsi* and *frustror* were separate species, and Bailey classified *mearnsi* as a separate species also. Now, with the advantage of having hundreds and even thousands of specimens to study, it is apparent that they are merely sub-species (if that) of the durable, omnipresent, ubiquitous coyote. My four years of battling *texensis* as an official of the Predator and Rodent Control Branch of the Fish and Wildlife Service revealed to me two characteristics for *texensis:* a very great reproductive potential and extreme adaptability. Most authorities agree that *texensis* is an intergrade between *mearnsi* and *frustror.* I call this attitude progress, because I believe that all races of *Canis latrans* are simply intergrades and that there is no true sub-speciation.

(6) *Canis latrans lestes* claims its homeland in Utah, Nevada, western Wyoming, and western Montana, Idaho, Oregon, and Washington east of the Cascades. It is commonly called the "mountain coyote" and has recently pushed its range northward to meet up with *incolatus*—in the "North to Alaska" movement. Although he admitted that there was certain intergradation with all of the sub-species whose territory surrounded it, Jackson still assigned 2,068 specimens to this sub-species when he did his monumental study. Color variations in this "mountain coyote" are extreme, and my opinion is that these variations are due to extreme variations in diet and in temperature ranges, rather than to differences in speciation. Remember that mine is a layman's view on this subject . . . a layman who feels that there is really only one species of coyote, only *Canis latrans.*

(7) *Canis latrans umpquensis* claims that narrow strip of territory west of the coastal range of mountains in Oregon and Washington. Jackson only had 45 specimens to put in this narrow sub-species class, and could not say whether or not they were intergraded with the more numerous *ochropus* sub-species south of it, or with the rare coyote of the heavily wooded coastal British Columbia. Jackson had no specimens from that area at all, and even today the coyote is a rarity there. Here there seems to be something of an argument for the validity of color determinants, as this coyote does seem to uniformly offer a darker, blacker, appearance than the sub-species whose territories it abuts.

176

(8) *Canis latrans ochropus,* is the California Valley Coyote, the animal found in California west of the Sierra Nevadas, to the Pacific Coast, south through central California to about 33° of north latitude. To my untutored mind, there is almost no difference worthy of mention between this coyote and the next subspecies to be named, the *clepticus.* Strangely enough, this coyote was described by Eschsholtz on his voyage with Kotzebue, way back in 1824—when there was no political border between the United States' California and Mexico's Baja California, yet the artificial border between the two subspecies is almost the same as today's existing border. One would have to assume that this sub-species provided the individuals which killed a human child in California. It should also be pointed out that this coyote is listed as "medium sized."

(9) *Canis latrans clepticus,* called the San Pedro Martir coyote, because most of its specimens were taken from the San Pedro Martir mountains on Baja California's rugged peninsula. This coyote is found only in San Diego County in the states, but its range extends southward only to about El Rosario, in Baja California. Again, I find no significant differences between this subspecies and those to both north and south—at least, no differences that could not be better explained by their environment. This coyote seems to be a creature of the high mountains, with a substantially different diet than that enjoyed by the lowlands coyotes to both sides of it.

(10) *Canis latrans peninsulae,* the coyote which occupies the rest of the long Baja peninsula is listed as being "similar to *clepticus,*" to which I say a hearty "Amen." Much of the claim for being different is based on dentition, which is described as being "heavier." Yet, when we remember that only 43 specimens were examined to bolster the claim for its being a different species, this becomes much less significant. Again the total impression is one of "medium-sized" coyotes, exactly the same as those others which are described from farther north. There is no physical barrier between *ochropus, clepticus,* and *peninsulae*—and very little reason for calling them separate sub-species. Intergradation is markedly apparent to those of us who have enjoyed the sport of calling coyotes to the gun on the Baja Peninsula.

(11) *Canis latrans mearnsi,* occupies a big piece of territory including all of Arizona and parts of Utah, Nevada, New Mexico, Chihuahua, and Sonora. This coyote is called the smallest of all, except for *Canis latrans microdon* which occupies a very limited area on the Texas-Mexico border near the Gulf of Mexico. *C.l.*

mearnsi's dentition is much smaller than most of the northern races of coyotes, but still larger than *microdon*. There is a great degree of intergradation occurring with *lestes, microdon,* and *texensis.*

(12) *Canis latrans jamesi,* the Tiburon Island coyote, is a very interesting case. Its type locality is Tiburon Island in the midriff of the Sea of Cortez. Here, surely, there is reason to believe in the existence of different characteristics due to an isolated environment. The coyote is a strong swimmer, but I doubt that any could swim to the mainland from Tiburon, or make the trip in the other direction. How they got to this island, with its 4,500 foot mountains pointing straight into the sky from mile deep waters, is a mystery to me. Evolution has produced very different iguanas on the isolated Galapagos; evolution has produced rattlesnakes without rattles on some isolated islands of the Sea of Cortez; and evolution has produced a chuckwalla found nowhere else on this world. We can logically expect a totally different sub-species of coyote in an isolated environment—but we are disappointed. The *jamesi* sub-species has perhaps the weakest claim to separate status of any coyote. It is described as being "apparently paler and more grayish than average *mearnsi,* longer eared than average *mearnsi,* skull about as in *mearnsi,* molariform teeth apparently somewhat heavier." Jackson only saw one specimen of this race and he was very dubious of its claim to separate status. Having watched the remarkable coyotes of Tiburon Island at fairly close range on several occasions, I would say that I see absolutely no difference between this coyote and the mainland races nearest to it. In fact, the environment of Tiburon Island is almost exactly the same as the environment of the nearby mainland (9 to 26 miles). The biggest difference is in the almost total absence of fresh water on the island. However, this does not mean that the clever coyote has learned to live without fresh water at all; the clever coyote has learned how to find fresh water wherever it exists, even on forbidding Tiburon Island.

(13) *Canis latrans microdon,* as its name implies, is a small-toothed small-bodied coyote found in a very small area. It has been identified from Nuevo Leon, Tamaulipas in Mexico and Cameron, Starr, and Hidalgo counties in Texas. This is an area with lots of small bird and mammal life, of bountiful food for the coyote, which makes me wonder why the type coyote is a small one. On the other hand, the whitetail deer of the hill country in Texas are among the smallest deer of their family found anywhere—perhaps showing that the size factor is hooked to

another interesting theory. There is some evidence to suggest that a hot climate forces the species to develop a smaller mass in relation to total surface area. If this is true, then the tiny *microcon* has a very large skin surface area and a very small total mass. When I first made the acquaintance of *microdon* in 1959, I thought I was looking at an immature coyote—even though the December data made that unlikely. When I asked if it were possible that these were immatures, veteran trappers told me, "That's all the bigger they get down here." Another thing that surprises me when I look back is the fact that we had several instances of coyotes killing calves in this area. The smallest race of coyotes was a calf-killing race, despite the abundance of rodent food. My notebooks from 1959 and 1961, when I worked the Texas area for the U.S. Fish and Wildlife Service Branch of Predator and Rodent Control substantiate this idea. Hartley Jackson only had 11 specimens of this smallest race to work with, yet I would agree with him that this smallest coyote has a good argument for sub-species status. It will be interesting to see if the constant characteristic of small size holds up as *microdon* continues to intergrade with *texensis* and *mearnsi* and *imparvidus*.

(14) *Canis latrans impavidus*, the Durango coyote, is identified as coming from the Pacific Coast slopes of Mexico, including the bottom end of Sonora, southwestern Chihuahua, western Durango and Zacatecas, and all of Sinaloa. Another medium-sized race of coyotes, Jackson theorized that this is an intergradation between *mearnsi* and *cagottis*, the so-called Mexican coyote.

(15) *Canis latrans cagottis*, is the Mexican coyote, but I find no reason to make it a sub-species at all. If we continue the steady intergradation tendency found as we leave the realm of *mearnsi*, on through *impavidus*, and into *cagottis*, differences would appear to be environmental-caused, due to differing diets and elevations.

(16) *Canis latrans vigilis*, the Colima coyote, was given sub-species status as the result of examining five specimens from a huge geographic area on the western side of the central America peninsula. Although it would be logical to say that this coyote is an extension of the *cagottis*, some differences in dentition made this impossible for Jackson. I submit that the limited evidence of five specimens is not enough to list it separately, that variations within species and sub-species are greater, individual to individual, than the characteristic differences listed here.

(17) *Canis latrans goldmani*, the Chiapas coyote, also listed on the basis of one specimen—which is not sufficient to list any

subspecies. However, this one specimen was much larger than any known race (or sub-species) of Mexican coyote. Somehow or another, coyote taxonomists have gotten into the habit of saying that this is the coyote common to Guatemala. Based on one specimen?

(18) *Canis latrans hondurensis*, the Honduras coyote, known only from four specimens, is much smaller than *goldmani*. When Goldman published the original description, he wrote, "It is possible that *Canis hondurensis* will eventually require reduction to sub-specific status under the wide ranging *Canis latrans,* but. . . ." This is further proof of Goldman's intelligence. However, I would question even sub-specific status.

(19) *Canis latrans dickeyi*, the Salvador coyote, the last subspecies given such separate status by Jackson, was identified based on two specimens collected in San Salvador. Jackson says that *dickeyi* is slightly larger than any of the known races of Mexican coyotes.

The arguments will continue to range for many years as to the validity of different status for different races, or family groups of coyotes. However, if we can accept the fact that our human genus and race includes individuals which vary to greater degrees than we have been able to sort out in the coyote race, then I would say that the following principle should apply:

If it is smaller than a red wolf, yet looks like the wolves of North America, it is a coyote. If it walks like a coyote, and howls like a coyote, it is a coyote.

If you cannot accept the epitome of togetherness that I espouse —that of calling all coyotes *Canis latrans,* and letting it go at that—then I suggest that we simplify things by this method:

Canis latrans ochropus should include all coyotes on the western coast of our continent from northern California through the southern tip of Baja. This would eliminate *clepticus* and *peninsulae.*

Canis latrans jamesi should be eliminated entirely. Further study of the coyotes on Tiburon island will undoubtedly tell us which sub-species they really belong in. The island is now a national park in Mexico, which may help the coyote to survive, or it may spell its doom.

Further study of the four Mexican-Central American races which Jackson labelled as *cagottis, vigilis, goldmani,* and *dickeyi,* and investigation of the possibility that *hondurensis* was simply an abberant individual, will probably tell us that all five of these sub-species can be lumped under the mantle of *goldmani.*

I further suggest that intergradation between *microdon* and *texensis* will undoubtedly eliminate any need to list a separate race known as *microdon*. It must be very difficult for the tiny Rio Grande coyote family to maintain any kind of genetic purity when they are surrounded by a sea of *texensis*. It's a wise coyote indeed that knows its own father. Strange families, such as *microdon*, are doomed to disappearance under current conditions.

A case can be made—although a slim one—for the existence of separate sub-species known as *incolatus*, *thamnos*, *lestes*, and *frustror*, along with old typical himself, *Canis latrans latrans*.

These changes would leave us with about eight separate sub-species of coyote. If this adaptable species continues to occupy the entire North American continent without big breaks between territories, the tendency would be toward more homogenization, rather than specialization. Perhaps when the final roll is called on North American wildlife, there will be only one coyote—the clever, adaptable, survivable, intelligent, and persevering coyote.

This coyote learned to mooch tidbits from tourists, in Jasper National Park, Canada.

Chapter 26

The Nature of the Beast

Is the coyote a ravenous killer of livestock, or a devoted parent seeking to feed its young? Is it a skulking predator that steals from man that which man intended to keep for himself, or is the coyote a necessity in the scheme of things we often call the web of life? Let's look at a few indicators of coyote behavior. You draw your own conclusions.

In 1981, in Los Angeles county, coyotes attacked and killed three-year-old Kelly Keene near her home in Glendale, California. Robert Keene, the child's parent, reported that this was the third time that coyotes had attacked one of his children near their home, just seven miles from downtown Los Angeles.

The director of the Los Angeles County Department of Animal Care and Control told me of two other attacks on small children in the past two years. One of these attacks occurred in Pomona, east of Los Angeles and one more at Agoura, which is in the northwestern sector of the big county.

Los Angeles county is completely closed to the discharge of all firearms. Thus, the coyote has had no need for its normal fear of man. In addition, residents have been feeding the coyotes. These animals have been "tamed" and lost their natural fear of humans. "Familiarity breeds contempt" may be the best description of the change in the Los Angeles coyote attitude toward men.

Obviously, the problem could be solved by allowing the use of shotguns in the area. With almost no danger to humans, the shotgun could quickly restore the coyote's normal fear of man.

Like Yellowstone Park's panhandling bears, coyotes lose their fear when fed by humans. Many years ago in Jasper National Park we photographed an adult coyote that had learned that tourists were a good source of food. He posed for his picture in return for goodies tossed out of the windows of tourists' cars. It would be only a question of time before that coyote decided to take a nip out of some child tourist, we imagined.

The Los Angeles county incident—which stands almost alone in literature—makes several important points. First of all, it proves the adaptability of coyotes, their ability to live with man, dine from man's table, and prosper while doing it. Secondly, coyotes are not being forced out of existence by the attack of urban sprawl—man's concrete does not intimidate clever coyotes. Furthermore, conditioning can change the inherited fears of countless generations. Association with humans is dangerous for humanity, and perhaps also for coyotes.

It should be mentioned again that these coyotes in Los Angeles county are certainly not the norm. Rather they are amazing exceptions to normal coyote behavior. Such aberrations are apt to increase as man takes over more and more of the earth for his own uses—crowding less adaptable species out and changing the behavior of the most adaptable of them all, coyotes.

Playful coyotes?

I saw a completely different facet of the coyote's varied behavior one April day in the Black Hills of South Dakota. Spring had come with a rush that year, and sheepmen were anxious to move their flocks up onto the national forest and off of badly mistreated winter pastures. I was working with government trapper George Barnes. We decided to check out the coyote sign ahead of the flocks which would soon move up into the higher country.

Using George's four wheel drive, we negotiated the melting snow and slippery slopes into high country which hadn't seen a human in four month's time. I always enjoyed my sojourns with George, because he was a good outdoorsman, an expert shot with his .270, and a good tracker—one of the best I'd met up north. We were riding along with the windows open, enjoying the balmy air. George maneuvered the rig onto a point of rocks that afforded a view of the country spread out to the east. Leaning against the front of the truck, we glassed the slopes below us until we spotted a strange sight—a flock of sheep working its way up into the mouth of a big draw that funneled up to right below us. A sheepherder's wagon, pulled by horses, labored along behind them.

"His grazing permit don't allow him to be up here for 'most a month," George said, "but he's all out of grass down by Interior (a place near the South Dakota Badlands), so he's moving up to give his sheep lots of green stuff at lambing time." Parentheses my own.

Most of the sheep were moving slowly, nipping at bits of grass that stuck up through the melting snow. But a few were well out in front, forging steadily up the trail as if anxious to reach their summer homes. One old ewe, a born leader, was fifty yards in front of the others. Suddenly, George whispered, "Lookit the coyote!"

Looking bigger'n life in his winter coat, the coyote had come out into the open meadow directly below us, about 150 yards distant. He walked deliberately to a big rock beside the trail, then crouched down behind it. His eyes were fixed on the trail where the advancing flock was due to appear.

"I've never actually seen a coyote kill a sheep," George whispered, "so let's watch."

The ewe purposefully advanced, coming up the trail worn three inches deep in the scant mountain soil by years of sheep use. The coyote crouched even lower. When the ewe was within ten feet of him, the coyote sprang into action. He leaped up in the air and landed stiff-legged astride the trail. Every hair on his body stood erect! With a terrified bawl, the ancient ewe almost turned a somersault in the air in its haste to retreat. The ewe fell, scrambled up, and dashed madly down the trail, baa-ing in terror. The coyote never moved from its stiff-legged pose until she was out of sight. Then he slid in behind the rock again and crouched down, head up and alert.

"Well, I'll be damned," George whispered quietly, "let's see what comes next." Fifteen minutes went by, while another group of sheep came into view, moving slowly up the trail straight for the coyote laying in ambush. Again he repeated the performance, suddenly bouncing out to straddle the path, and sending the terrified sheep bawling back down the hill.

After the third performance, I whispered, "That coyote doesn't want to kill a sheep this time."

"He ain't never going to get the chance," George answered, and his .270 roared. At that easy range, the coyote was a "gift" target, and George didn't often miss. I have to admit that I kind of hated to see that one killed. Coyotes with a sense of humor are rare.

Eating the Victim While Still Alive

One of the most distressing habits of the coyote, shared by many other carnivores, is that of eating its dinner while the dinner is still alive. Obviously, it would be wrong to ascribe human emotions to the coyote, so we will not say that the coyote is cruel or sadistic—but rather, acknowledge that he is just doing his thing, doing what comes naturally.

A respected observer of the wildlife scene, Victor Cahalane, reported in the February 1947 issue of the *Journal of Mammalogy* a bizarre incident of coyote versus deer which he had observed on a national park in Arizona. He watched as three coyotes pulled down one mule deer doe out of a herd of eight deer, and began eating the hindquarters while the deer struggled to get up. Interestingly, another doe rushed to the rescue—or tried to—and made a heroic frontal assault on the coyotes, driving them away from the partially eaten, but still alive, doe. When coyotes tried to attack the rescuer deer, nipping at her exposed hindquarters, she was driven from the battle field.

The three coyotes then began to fight among themselves, and two of them were driven away from the still living deer by the oldest coyote. That coyote then continued to feed on the hindquarters of the living deer, which finally died from severe loss of blood. The other two coyotes then came back to the scene and finished eating the deer. Twenty-four hours after the killing, only scattered hair remained to tell the tale.

Although this well documented account wasn't written until 1947, one should not assume that this was a new behavior pattern for the coyote. Unlike the killing of the child, this was definitely not a first for the coyote clan.

Back in February of 1926, F. M. Dragatt reported in *Outdoor Life* magazine that coyotes were killing many deer on the winter ice in the state of Washington. Commenting on the nasty table manners of the coyotes, Dragatt added this paragraph:

"I have seen trails of (deer) blood covering two acres on the ice where a poor deer, after it had been broken down, still tried to get away by dragging itself back and forth across the ice while the coyotes were eating out of the hindquarters."

We cannot explain this "eat them alive" habit of the coyote by saying that he really likes his meat fresh. We have seen too many instances of the coyote dining on very ripe carrion, without worrying about the maggots, the stench, or the fact that the meat was "melted down" to the point where it no longer resembled meat.

Dangerous killer of human children, playful goblin of unwanted sheep dinners, merciless killer that eats its prey alive—there are many facets of the coyote psyche that are worthy of mention. But the main lesson to be learned is that the coyote has a complex personality, unpredictable except for one or two traits, such as intelligence and adaptability. Those two it possesses in abundance.

This same vicious killer is a solicitous, careful, conscientious parent which does an excellent job of rearing its young and of preparing them for life in the cruel world that awaits them. When food is very scarce, the parent coyotes will still bring food to the pups, even to the point of almost starving themselves. The female seems to have sufficient milk for even the largest litter, although she may be reduced to a bag of bones herself. One of the best wildlife parents I've ever encountered was the female coyote in Stutsman County, North Dakota.

While a high school freshman in North Dakota, I spent a lot of spare time roaming the prairies. I attained the rank of Kit Carson and Dan'l Boone in the eyes of my classmates when I discovered a coyote den a few miles south of town. Determined to learn a lot about coyotes and figuring correctly that the pelts were worthless anyway, I decided against trying to capture the coyotes, but rather to watch the coyote family as it grew up.

However, I couldn't resist the temptation to prove my great "coyote finding" ability to my classmates by taking them out to see the coyote den and to listen at the mouth of the den in the hope that they, too, would hear the sounds of coyote pups at play below. The greatly increased human activity worried the mother coyote and she responded by moving the entire litter of five pups to a second den, located about half a mile to the south. We embryonic trackers figured out what had happened when we found the female's track—and beside it a set of tiny pup tracks—on some soft sand half-way between the two dens. With that evidence, we began to circle out looking for the new den. We found it. In our ignorance of coyote denning habits, we decided that this must be a short tunnel den, because "she wouldn't have had time to dig a deeper one, and there wasn't much fresh dirt showing on top."

The fact that the coyote hadn't dug anything, but had just cleaned out another badger tunnel was lost on us. Certain that we had a short job ahead of us, we brought out two shovels and dug hard for three hours, without getting any sight of pups or the end of the tunnel. It was getting dark so we left. So did the coyotes; she moved her entire litter between darkness and dawn. It took us three days to find the new den. To make the story short, our activities forced the coyote family to move four separate times. She may have moved still once more; we don't know, for we lost the coyote family completely for two months. In late August I once again caught sight of the family—Mother Coyote and five fat big pups, all busily hunting mice along the twisting length of a small watercourse that ran through the middle of a big pasture. I went to the farmer who owned the pasture and asked him for permission to trap coyotes in his pasture that coming winter. I didn't tell him that I'd seen six coyotes, because I was afraid that he might ask for a share of the expected profits.

He responded by laughing me out of the yard. "I haven't seen a coyote on this farm in ten years, kid!" That coyote family lived to a ripe old age on his land, without the farmer ever even knowing that they were there. He didn't, however, raise sheep.

Just as the picture of a coyote eating a still living doe is the very epitome of all that is bad about the coyote; so also the picture of a coyote mother carrying her pup in her teeth, moving it to a safer, or more comfortable, den is the epitome of all that is admirable about the coyote.

Coyote Relationships with Other Species

How does the coyote get along with other kinds of wildlife which share its world with it? Let's consider only wildlife forms that are not the coyote's food items. This cuts down the subject area considerably.

Coyotes and bobcats are neighbors over much of the coyote range, and there is little love lost between them. Almost every government trapper has at least one story about coyotes chasing bobcats up a tree and of keeping them there for hours and hours. The adult bobcat is a fearsome adversary in a fight, and I cannot imagine that the coyote would willingly run into that buzzsaw of teeth and claws. However, coyotes chase bobcats in much the same way that domestic dogs chase domestic cats. In most cases, the domestic dog comes out of it much the worse-for-wear when he tangles with an adult house cat of even half his size. The literature documents bobcats having been killed by coyotes; so it does happen. However, the bobcat's ability to climb trees probably saves it from having to fight for its life. Most bobcat-coyote encounters end with the bobcat treed. However, trappers curse the coyote for its habit of killing and tearing to shreds a trapped bobcat it finds. Sometimes the coyote eats the bobcat flesh, but there are times when it simply tears the trapped animal to shreds without feeding.

The large wolf, the timber or lobo wolf, is an avowed enemy of the coyote, although they are close generic relatives. I figure that the coyote was able to extend its range northward to Alaska only after the larger wolf was eliminated over much of that range. When the big wolf was present, coyotes kept a mighty low

The badger is about the only animal which seems (at times) to get along with the coyote.

profile, for the bigger wolf could catch them and often kill and eat the smaller predator.

The badger is a very different story. There has been some kind of a tacit partnership between *some* coyotes and *some* badgers. Many observers have reported seeing a badger and a coyote traveling as a team, cooperating in the digging out of burrowing rodents, and even sharing the food supply amicably. This is no recent phenomena, for pre-Columbian pottery has been found showing the coyote and badger in close partnership. In fact, the usually emotionless, stoic coyote has been observed cavorting about its badger companion like a playful pup and engaging in grooming and licking behavior with the badger.

You will note that I said that *some* individuals of the coyote and badger clans have acted this way. Other situations bring other results. According to a case reported in Wyoming, tracks showed that a badger had found a coyote den, eaten the heads off of the nine pups and departed, leaving the rest of the carcass uneaten.

There are many cases of Golden eagles swooping down and (seemingly) attacking coyotes. I put in the qualifier "seemingly" as I am not aware of any eagles actually killing a coyote, and I think that task beyond the abilities of the bird. It is my impression, without any solid backing, that the eagle is simply in a playful mood, using its greater speed and safe position in the air to bedevil the coyote. In contrast, I have twice seen Golden eagles and coyotes both feeding on (large) carrion animals. In both cases, the two species seemed to ignore each other in the presence of plentiful dinners. I have also seen Golden eagles stuff themselves so full of carrion that they were unable to fly until digestive processes reduced the load. In these situations, the coyote was also present and made no attempt to attack the very vulnerable eagle.

Chapter 27

The Coyote in Nature's Scheme

Before research proved otherwise, it was once popular in the United States to speak of a "Balance of Nature" and talk of a perfect situation wherein predators—such as the coyote—controlled the numbers of a prey species—such as the cottontail rabbit or the prairie dog. According to this theory, the coyote would dine on the rodent until low rodent numbers make it no longer worthwhile for the coyote to make a living off of that particular rodent. This was the case of reaching the point of diminishing returns.

Careful observers always had trouble with this sort of reasoning. As long as fifty years ago, they began to advance the opposite theory—that the availability of rodent prey controlled the numbers of predators in a given area. They pointed out that the reproductive potential of the rodent was very high; that of the coyote relatively low. When rodent numbers periodically irrupted, the rodent banquet lured great numbers of predators—raptors and terrestrial meat-eaters. However, these meat-eaters increased slowly and couldn't keep up with the great reproductive potential of the rodents.

One of the most interesting situations along this line occurred in Texas in 1957–1960, when the common cotton rat—*Sigmodon hispidus* staged a population explosion of monumental proportions. Across a great expanse of Texas, including the winter

There are four mule deer in this picture. Can you find them? Wildlife research in many western states has convicted the coyote as being a depressing influence upon mule deer numbers. Greatest loss is to fawns in the first two weeks of their life.

garden area famed for its truck garden crops, the cotton rat became so numerous that it was no longer possible to use mechanical harvesters for many crops—because the bodies of the cotton rats became part of the harvested crop.

The area of greatest population increase included counties in which the Branch of Predator and Rodent Control of the Bureau of Sport Fisheries and Wildlife had begun intensive programs aimed at reducing coyote numbers, and counties in which there were no organized control programs. In both areas the cotton rat increased in numbers, at exactly the same astronomical rate. The infestations continued for the same length of time—in areas of coyote control and in no control areas alike.

The explosion reached the "boom and bust" stage—in controlled and uncontrolled areas alike—at the same time. The cotton rat in both areas became not only scarce, but almost unknown.

While this cotton rat irruption was in progress, meat eaters of all kinds migrated into the area of easy eating from all sides, and fed to their hearts content, becoming fat and prosperous. But they did not make a significant dent in the rodent population. When the cotton rats died out, the predators searched elsewhere.

Availability of prey determined predator numbers. Predation had not controlled a rodent population. But does predation have an effect upon populations of game animals; species which have roughly the same, or lower reproductive potential as the coyote has?

One of the most interesting pieces of research on that question is the research project by Don J. Neff and Norman G. Woolsey, *Special Report No. 8* (published under provisions of the Federal Aid in Wildlife Restoration Act Project W–78–R, Work Plan 2 Job 16) dated November of 1979. The Arizona biologists studied the pronghorned antelope population on Anderson Mesa. This herd had once been the largest in Arizona but had dropped from over 2,200 animals in the early 1930s to an average of only 456 animals according to aerial survey counts of 1961–1978. The Anderson Mesa study area is a basalt-capped plateau extending south and east from Flagstaff, Arizona for about forty miles.

Unlike most predator-prey studies, where the human activity of gathering the data directly influences animal behavior and thus gives a bias to the results, the Anderson Mesa study was accomplished for the most part with unobtrusive distant observation. A "spy-tower" was built and manned for long periods of time to record antelope and coyote activity. Accurate information about the mortality of antelope fawn was gained by using a pair of dogs, trained to scent out any remains and lead the biologists to the remains. In the case of coyote-killed antelope fawns, the remains are usually only a handful of hair and a few bone chips. Without the dog's sensitive nose, the human observer would seldom find these scant remains.

The following are quotations from the report:

Fawn Survival and 1080 Coyote Control

The response of antelope fawn survival rates to incidence of coyote control with toxicants strongly suggests that coyote predation has been a major factor in fawn survival for more than 30 years. Compound 1080 was first used in 1948 in Unit 5B. In 1946 primary reliance was on strychnine drop baits. Minimum fawn survival with 1080 coyote control was 67 percent, which was much greater than the maximum fawn survival experienced without control work. In Table 4, years are grouped into three categories: control work done the previous winter, control work done a year earlier, and no control work done for two or more years. The fawn survival means of these three treatment groups are significantly different.

Relationship of pronghorn antelope fawn survival to coyote control in present Game Management Unit 5B, 1944 to 1978. Data are fawns per one hundred does based on June or July aerial surveys.

Control work during preceding winter		One year since last control work		Two or more years since last control work	
1946	62	1947	66	1944	30
1948	74	1951	62	1945	39
1949	79	1953	57	1956	62
1950	90	1955	66	1957	32
1952	81	1960	48	1958	34
1954	71			1961	28
1959	80			1962	22
1966	69			1963	48
1967	67			1964	48
1969	93			1965	23
1970	74			1971	55
				1972	46
				1974	44
				1975	30
				1976	21
				1977	28
				1978	28
				1979	14

11 years	6 years	17 years
Mean survival rate of fawns . . . 76.4 per 100 does.	59.0 per 100 does	33.9 per 100 does

Note: Coyote control work consisted of placement of poison baits by U.S. Fish and Wildlife Service personnel: strychnine in 1946 and 1080 thereafter.

Two years, 1968 and 1973 were excluded from this table because of severe winter weather which affected subsequent fawn survival.

The table tells us the following: When coyotes were killed during the winter preceding the birth of antelope fawns, 76.4 percent fawns survived through the summer's aerial count. When a full year elapsed between coyote poisoning and the fawning

194

season, only 59 fawns survived through the aerial count time. When two or more years elapsed between coyote poisoning and the fawning season, the average dropped all the way down to 33.9 percent of the fawns surviving through the aerial count time. In 1979, if I read the results correctly, only 14 percent of the fawns survived. In 1979, there had been no coyote poisoning since 1971. Given eight years in which to build up their numbers, coyotes in 1979 claimed so many fawn dinners that only 14 fawns survived per one hundred. Remember that most adult antelope does produce twin fawns. In some areas, and some research studies, one hundred does produced one hundred eighty fawns. But maybe a great part of antelope fawn mortality goes unnoticed . . . as the report continues:

In spite of a large crew in the field during fawning, Larsen (1970) in New Mexico was not able to find much direct evidence of fawn mortality. In the final report on that study, Montoya (1972) reported only one fawn kill at a coyote feeding site. In the present study we were able to improve the score, thanks to the hounds. A total of 40 neonatal fawn kills at coyote feeding sites were found in three fawning seasons. One fawn kill by a coyote was observed just after the hunting season in September. Six instances were found of coyotes killing adult antelope. Sites of adult kills showed unmistakable evidence of desperate battle (rocks rolled, grass and soil torn up, tufts of hair scattered about) which was not present in several cases where antelope had been shot and later were consumed by coyotes.

Based on doe counts from aerial surveys and assuming a natality rate of at least 150 percent, at least 336 fawns were born in the Pine Hill study area during the first three years of work. If we assume that the 98 fawns counted on aerial surveys represented the total for the area, then 238 fawns (71 percent) failed to survive. Only 41 of the 238 missing fawns were accounted for, leaving about 83 percent of the fawn mortality unexplained. For the entire six year study, fawn natality and mortality estimates suggest a loss of 62 to 85 percent of the fawns.

Mortality factors other than coyote predation cannot be ruled out, but in 865 fawn observations during this study, we have never seen one that was sick, weak, injured, or otherwise abnormal. It must be concluded that at this time coyote predation is the predominant cause of fawn mortality. . . .

*   *   *

During the nine years since the antelope herd recovered from the 1967 winter die-off, the total population has remained relatively stable, ranging from about 330 to 480 animals each year. During this period a total of 330 bucks have been taken legally, while total cumulative survey counts have been 692 bucks and 1,906 does. Total legal harvest, thus represents 12.7 percent of the total adult population and 47.7 percent of the total cumulative buck count.

During this same period, the cumulative total of 1,906 does could be expected to have produced at least 150 fawns per 100 does, or a total production of 2,859 fawns. Aerial surveys counted a cumulative total of 732 fawns, leaving 2,127 fawns unaccounted for, or a loss of 74 percent of the fawns projected.

The number of fawns probably produced and lost is more than 6 times the number of bucks harvested legally. (Emphasis supplied by the author.)

A total of 65 winter and 102 spring–summer scats have been analyzed. Results show that cottontails and jackrabbits are the most important food item on the winter range, followed by cattle (probably mostly carrion, but possibly including some calves), rodents, and woodrats. Antelope and mule deer material showed up in 9 and 12 percent of the scats respectively and probably included both kills and carrion. Insects, reptiles and birds were rare, while juniper berries and other vegetation were common items.

On the spring fawning grounds, scats were mostly collected during fawning observations and kill searches. It is not surprising that 63 percent of the scats contained antelope remains. Cattle and other big game were minor elements as were rabbits. Rodent material was found in 28 percent of the scats, indicating considerable time spent mouse hunting. Birds were also a major item coming from nesting horned larks and meadowlarks. Insects were present in 25 percent of the scats, and again, juniper berries and other vegetation were common.

It must be concluded that the coyotes present on the fawning grounds were not there coincidentally; they were hunting and taking antelope, both adults and fawns. The actual killing of a fawn was observed only twice, but a total of 35 coyotes were seen at 20 fresh antelope kills, both adult and fawn, during the course of the study. In the country east of the Mesa, scats collected from fall through late winter show the kind of rabbit-rodent diet that would be expected, along with carrion from larger animals. No special effort was made to find antelope kills on the winter range, but two adult kills by coyotes are known.

* * *

Rabbits and rodents are major coyote prey items throughout much of the year. High populations of small mammals can probably support a high coyote population when they could have a drastic impact on antelope fawn survival during a few short weeks in spring. Assessment of the coyote-antelope situation, therefore, requires a general understanding of rabbit and rodent population trends.

In a part of their conclusions, the researchers wrote the following paragraph:

Abundant evidence has been obtained of coyote predation, including direct observation of coyote killing and feeding behavior, interactions between coyotes and mother does, physical evidence at kill sites and coyote scat analyses. A high rate of antelope fawn survival in the past has been observed to follow the control of coyotes with compound 1080 baits. The same kind of effect was reproduced on a small scale at Pine Hill in 1977 by intensive steel trapping. It must be concluded that coyote predation on neonatal fawns is the major cause of the high rate of fawn loss in the Anderson Mesa antelope herd. In turn, inadequate fawn recruitment appears to be the primary cause of the low antelope population. Factors contributing to this excessive coyote predation include lack of tall cover in which fawns can bed and hide, high coyote densities, and the observed fact that many coyotes are experienced hunters of fawns and actively seek them as prey.

This *Special Report No. 8* has much more to say about the coyote-antelope relationship, and it is recommended for further study by the serious student of the coyote and his place in the environment.

Another interesting investigation of the effect of coyote predation upon game animal numbers is given in *Wildlife Research Report Number 10* (published by the Oregon Department of Fish and Wildlife) entitled: *Mortality of Mule Deer Fawns in Southeastern Oregon, 1968–1979.* This report was financed by Pittman-Robertson and the investigators were Charles E. Trainer, James C. Lemos, T. P. Kistner, William C. Lightfoot, and Dale E. Toweill. Some interesting quotes from the report are listed here:

The study areas were located on Steens Mountain, a large fault-block mountain lying eighty kilometers south of Burns in southeastern Oregon. . . . Coyotes were the principal carnivores on study areas, although bobcats, cougars *(Felis concolor),* and Golden eagles were also present. Cougars were rare, but were sighted . . . two times during the study. . . . Miniaturized battery-powered radio transmitters attached to breakaway collars were used to instrument deer in this study. . . .

An assessment of the effect of coyote removal on fawn mortality from all causes was conducted between January 1976 and the end of the study in the spring of 1979. In this effort, coyotes were removed from the Frazier Field winter range. No program of coyote control was conducted on the P. Hill winter range, which was used for comparative purposes.

Helicopter gunning for coyotes was used for all coyote removals in the control program. Use of toxicants on federal lands and in federal programs was banned by President Nixon's Executive Order 11643 in 1972, and programs associated with winter access on the study area largely precluded the use of leghold traps or M-44 devices. Aerial gunning of coyotes has the added advantage of removing coyotes that might be "trap shy" and of being selective for the target species.

Coyote removal efforts were conducted under provisions of a cooperative agreement between the Oregon Department of Fish and Wildlife and the U.S. Fish and Wildlife Service. . . . U.S. Fish and Wildlife personnel flew as gunners on all coyote removal flights . . . semi-automatic shotguns with #4 buck-shot were used to kill coyotes. . . . Coyote removal flights were begun 17 January 1976 and continued through March 1976. In each of the three subsequent winters (1976–1977 through 1978–1979) coyote removal flights were begun in November and continued through at least March. In 1977, coyote removal flights were conducted as late as May.

Causes of mortality by season among mule deer fawns that died on Steens Mountain 1971 through 1979.

Season	Accident	Disease	Starvation	Coyote	Cat	Eagle	Undetermined
Summer	6	10	6	24	11	1	5
Fall	0	0	0	13	5	0	17
Winter (January thru April)	0	1	2	43	2	0	17

NOTE: These are the 163 mule deer fawns that wore the instruments and died by all causes during the study periods. If we substract the "undetermined" deaths from the total, we find that we have data on 124 "known" mortalities of mule deer fawns. Coyotes accounted for eighty of the known deaths, or 64.5 percent of the known deaths.

To quote further from the report of the Steens Mountain Study,

Effect of coyote removal on Coyote Numbers

A total of 536 coyotes were removed from the Frazier Field winter range (194 square kilometers) from January 1976 to March 1979. Numbers of coyotes removed each year ranged from 99 (0.5 coyotes per square kilometer) to 183 (0.9 coyotes per square kilometer). The maximum number of coyotes removed any one day was 45. In 1976, coyote removal began in January and continued through March; in later years, coyotes were shot intermittently from November to late March or May. . . .

Attempts to estimate coyote numbers on Steens Mountain study areas from 1970 through 1974 by scent-post and siren-response inventories proved unsatisfactory. Both techniques were abandoned because wind and/or precipitation often prevented implementation or completion of scheduled inventories, and because infrequent and highly variable coyote responses made it impossible to detect even large changes in coyote numbers.

Failure of these attempts necessitated the use of the cumulative rate of coyotes killed per hour of helicopter flight time as an index to coyote numbers. The cumulative rate was calculated at the end of each flight based on totals of coyotes taken and hours flown during all previous flights of that year. The effectiveness of this measurement of coyote abundance depended upon the assumption that the coyote kill rate fluctuated with coyote density. Beginning with the second winter of coyote control, the average removal rate of coyotes declined significantly during each successive winter that control was conducted.

Although the index of coyote removal decreased during 1976–1977 to 1978–1979, the age structure of coyotes taken each year showed no appreciable change. However, there was a slight increase in the relative percentage of individuals in the one to three year old class, from 71 percent in 1976, to 82 percent in 1976–1977, to 87 percent in both 1977–1978 and 1978–1979 samples. This increase was not interpreted as evidence of a lowering of age structure because of heavy exploitation. Rather it was attributed to a higher proportion of yearlings in the population during 1976–1977 than in other years because of increased reproductive success in 1976 or increased survival of pups through the mild winter of 1976–1977. No change in reproductive rates, as explained below, was detected during this study. The absence of significant change in age structure of coyotes during the four winters of control suggested that (1) aerial gunning was not selective for particular age classes of coyotes, and (2) that the control effort did not stimulate increased survival rates because of lowered population density. Because virtually all coyotes observed during helicopter flights were subsequently killed, we believed that decreases in removal rates on Frazier Field winter range during the study reflected reduced coyote numbers rather than reduced vulnerability of coyotes to aerial gunning. The recorded sex ratio of coyotes removed did not differ significantly from 1:1 for any of the four winter collection periods.

In summary, the cumulative removal rates of coyotes decreased significantly each year starting with the second winter of coyote control on Frazier Field winter range. We concluded that this decrease reflected a genuine reduction in coyote numbers. There was no measurable change in age structure or reproductive rate during the period of coyote control.

And again we quote from the Steens Mountain study, under their heading of

Effect of Coyote Removal on Fawn Mortality

... Based on herd composition counts, the mean rate of fawn mortality (51 percent) on Frazier Field area during winters before coyote removal was significantly greater than the mean (35 percent) during winters of control. The average winter loss (51 percent) among instrumented fawns before coyote removal was also much greater than the average (28 percent) during removal. . . .

These findings were consistent with our conclusion that coyote control did reduce fawn mortality on the Frazier Field winter range.

... During the period before coyote control, 48 percent of all fawn mortalities were attributed to coyote predation, compared with 50 percent during the period after coyote control was initiated. A greater proportion of losses due to starvation, accidents and disease was indicated during the years before coyote removal than was found following initiation of removal (22 percent versus 11 percent). This difference, however, was probably not related to control of coyotes.

Effect of Coyote Removal on Deer Numbers

Aerial deer inventories were flown by helicopter over Frazier Field and P. Hill Winter ranges in April of each year, 1977 through 1979, to determine if changes in numbers of mule deer occurred as a result of coyote control. The average number of deer observed on both winter ranges during each year was 1,212; 1,699; and 1,695. . . . Therefore, during the winter, the estimated increase in survival obtained by coyote removal was apparently adequate to maintain the deer population on Frazier Field winter range but was not sufficient to cause a measurable increase in deer numbers.

The authors of the Steens Mountain report wanted to make a valid comparison between results obtained in their study and the results of other studies on free-ranging herds of mule deer. They reported the following: In the Oak Creek, Utah study of 1947–1956, it was reported that coyote predation was involved in one-fourth of loss from birth to hunting season. In the Spanish Fork Canyon, Utah study of 1977 and 1978, **there was no coyote predation!** In the North Central Montana study of 1976 and 1977, coyotes were involved in nine of ten deaths reported. (It should be pointed out that this was a very limited study, with only a sample of 33 mortalities all told.) The South Central Washington study of 1976, which measured mule deer fawn mortality from birth to December, coyote predation caused three-fourths of the fawn loss during the first sixty days of their young lives, and coyotes were responsible for ten of fourteen deaths. These results compare with the Steens Mountain reported loss to coyote predation of 49 percent of the fawn crop.

To further put their own study results in perspective, the Oregon researchers compiled results of six studies of fawn mortality among white-tailed deer fawns. Five of these studies were conducted in Texas, and reported "at least 50 percent of loss due to coyotes," ... "40 percent of loss due to coyotes," ... "Coyote predation 67 percent of loss," ... "50 percent of loss due to predation—mostly by coyotes," ... "coyote and bobcat predation 97 percent of loss," that report coming from the Oklahoma Wichita Mountains study in 1974–1975. Oklahomans also conducted a 1970–1972 study in the Cookson Hills Refuge area, which reported that disease was a 71 percent cause of mortality due to blood loss and infection from lone star ticks. No mention was made of coyote losses in that study.

Going back to Oregon's Steens Mountain study, we find the following:

> Predation by coyotes was the major cause of fawn mortality during the current study. Coyotes accounted for 49 percent of all losses occurring between June and March and for 38, 37 and 66 percent of all losses during summer, fall, and winter seasons, respectively.
>
> Investigation of fawn losses in some other mule deer herds have also shown coyote predation to be a major cause of mortality.

The Oregon investigators compiled a very interesting table which shows that (with one inexplicable exception where coyote

202

removal actually resulted in a decrease in fawn production) coyote control methods paid remarkable dividends in total numbers of fawns produced per one hundred does.

What did it cost to achieve this increased survivability of fawns in the Oregon study? Quoting from their report:

> Costs associated with helicopter gunning of coyotes indicated that the net cost of each fawn surviving the winter as a result of coyote removal was about $30.38. At this rate, costs may not be excessive if the additional animals can be passed on to the hunter, as data from Robinette et al. (1977:116) suggest.

In conclusion, we agree with those who suggest that the ultimate factor limiting ungulate populations is habitat. Data from our study indicates, however, that predation was the primary factor limiting the size of the deer population on Steens Mountain . . . On Frazier Field winter range, coyote control was effective in decreasing fawn mortality, but probably only to the extent of offsetting adult losses. It appeared that more intensive coyote removal efforts would be needed to reduce predation sufficiently to allow the deer population to increase. If such a program was initiated, deer numbers would need to be closely monitored, so that harvest could be increased as herd size approached carrying capacity.

Let's talk about whitetailed deer now. Does coyote predation limit the size of deer herds? We were interested in the study conducted on the Rob and Bessie Welder Wildlife Foundation, near Sinton, Texas, performed by John G. Kie, Marshall White, and Frederick F. Knowlton, in 1973. The terse wording of the abstract of their research report is quoted here, in its entirety:

> High losses of newborn whitetailed deer fawns to coyote predation have been reported on the Welder Wildlife Refuge since the early 1960s. A coyote control program was initiated in 1973 within a 391 hectare study area to observe the effects of reducing predation pressure on deer population dynamics. Outside the predator exclosure the 1972–1978 average deer density was 34.6 per km^2. Predator control led to increases in fawn survival which resulted in an increase in population density to a peak of 84 deer per km^2. Immediate effects of these increased population densities included a decrease in the gross re-

productive rate and an increase in mortality in the three to twelve month age class. The result was a cessation of population growth but no immediate decline in deer numbers. Sex ratios among adult deer from 1974–1977 averaged 37 percent male inside and 24 percent male outside the exclosure. At these elevated population densities, the deer consumed a nutritionally suboptimal diet which may have predisposed them to observed increases in endoparasitism. Exclosure deer conceived later, retained antler velvet longer and shed hardened antlers earlier than other deer. Mortality of adult deer did not increase sufficiently to bring about a reduction in deer numbers until four to five years after the start of the predator control efforts.

I would like to add one comment on the Knowlton et al. study on the Welder Wildlife Refuge. The unnaturally high numbers of deer present on the area (both in the exclosure and in the control area outside the exclosure) probably makes it impossible to determine the long range results of a coyote removal program. In addition, the results are not reliable because the exclosure fence did not stop travel into and out of the exclosure by either coyotes or deer. These limitations were, of course, noted by the authors themselves in the complete wording of their report.

Another very interesting study of coyote predation on deer is found in the progress reports and final report of Project W–120–R–11. This report from Montana studied the situation along the

Whitetale deer fawns are vulnerable to coyote attack during their first few weeks of life.

breaks of the Missouri River in the vicinity of the Charles M. Russel National Wildlife Refuge. To quote from the report:

Coyotes apparently prey most on deer when more preferred food is scarce. Thus, deer become "buffer" species (not the traditional definition of buffer species) for coyotes. This situation allows some coyotes to survive at a higher rate than if they depended solely upon the major prey items; however, the population often declines, indicating that many are going short of food under these conditions. Reduced food could eliminate many coyotes and reduce reproduction for survivors which we apparently witnessed during 1976–1977. If coyote foods continue to follow abundance cycles of the providing species (voles, mice, rabbits, deer), deer appear to be less important to coyotes than are small mammals. It is not known whether changes in coyote social organization affect predation on deer. . . .

The deer population decline, attributed to the severe 1971–1972 winter, reduced deer density to approximately half their peak numbers (Hamlin 1979). The status of the coyote population and their predation on deer, before, during and after a peak still has not been studied. The high predation observed on adult deer during winter 1975–1976 (Knowles 1976) and fawns during summer 1976 and 1977 (Dood 1978) occurred during the low of the deer population cycle. Heavy, thick ground ice, which occurred during the otherwise relatively mild winter of 1975–1976 (Hamlin 1976) accompanied the highest observed winter predation on deer.

This research project gathered much valuable data about deer and coyote relationships, and is subject to many different interpretations. However, to report strictly what the researchers wanted to report, let us quote from the abstract, which serves as prelude to the job final report:

Coyote control accomplished the desired result of a minimum reduction of at least 50 percent of the precontrol population. Data on population levels of deer and antelope, as well as those of rabbits and rodents, are presented and discussed as they relate to population levels of, and predation by, coyotes. Coyotes can and do exert some short term control on deer and/or antelope populations in certain years and/or areas of Montana, but other factors ultimately control the long term population trends of these species. Under conditions existing during this study, it was concluded and recommended that coyote control is not justified and should not be carried out by this Department solely for the benefit of the deer or antelope populations.

Philip Schladweiler prepared the job final report on September 30, 1980, to summarize work accomplished under Project W–120–R–11 (5893). The publication is recommended to all serious students of the deer-vs-coyote question.

In a less serious vein, the student of coyotes is referred to the August, 1974 issue of the *National Geographic Magazine* (page 279). Hope Ryden presented the results of her long observation of the coyotes of the National Elk Refuge near Jackson, Wyoming. Although marred by anthropomorphic nonsense that gives human traits to wild coyotes, the article is a sensitive portrayal of the good side of the coyote as a devoted family animal. As one would expect of a *National Geographic* article, it is superbly illustrated with color photographs of the coyotes with their young. Ms. Ryden reports that the large litter sizes sometimes reported in the literature are usually the result of two or more females denning in the same den, and paints an interesting picture of a complex social organization including "baby-sitting" adults which are not the parents of the pups, but unattached adults taking a share of the duties of feeding young pups. Ms. Ryden draws the conclusion that coyotes normally mate for life.

On the last page of her *National Geographic* article Hope Ryden says, "But federal control agents, through intensified trapping and by hunting from airplanes and helicopters, reported that they had actually killed 10,000 more coyotes from June 1972 to June 1973 than in the previous year when poison was still in their arsenal. And even more recently, federal agencies have approved experimental and emergency use of a poisoning device called the M–44, shown to be relatively selective against coyotes. The future of *Canis latrans* could hardly look worse."

Remember that her article was written in late 1973 or early 1974. She felt that the future of the coyote, with so many weapons to eradicate him, was very bleak; thus Hope Ryden joined the long list of those who have studied the coyote a bit, and felt that he would suffer extinction. I am very happy to inform Hope Ryden that the coyote, whose future she worried about, is very much alive and well in 1983—a decade after she expressed her worry.

In fact, as the scientific research studies reported earlier will testify, the coyote is more numerous in 1983 than it was in 1973—in the both unnatural study area of the National Elk Refuge, and in the natural habitat outside the protection of the refuge in Montana and Wyoming. The coyote will gladly join Mark Twain, who responded to a news story reporting that he had died, with the words, "Stories of my death are greatly exaggerated." And that makes me happy, too.

Chapter 28

The Last Word

For most of recorded history, man has waged an unceasing war against coyotes. Man has won individual battles, but has never really endangered coyotes as a species—not anywhere, not at any time. The reason for coyotes' survivability is quite simple.

They seek to stay alive; man seeks to eliminate coyotes for the benefit of himself and other species—for the benefit of Princess Lamb and Prince Wool. No species will struggle as hard as coyotes struggle when their existence is at stake.

When man succeeded in reducing the coyote population to low levels—as he did in many states during the years when Compound 1080 was used—man loses his incentive. Losses to coyotes become very small; so man stops his efforts. He has reached the point of diminishing returns for his efforts. He can no longer kill many coyotes in a period of time; he must devote himself to the arduous task of "mopping up," trying to take the last few remaining individuals. Those surviving individuals are the smartest and most elusive of the breed because only the fittest have survived man's onslaught.

So man loses interest in the job or—and I prefer to believe this view—he does not really want to eliminate the coyote. Only the most callous sheeprancher who has lost his buttocks to the coyote would actually choose elimination. I have on hand a personal letter from a Beach, North Dakota rancher, which says in part, "I am a rancher who at one time ran from 450 to 500 head of ewes until the coyotes forced me to go to cows. I still have thirty ewes but don't put them out to pasture . . . . Not only are sheep being killed in my area, but there have been many incidents of newborn calves being killed . . . I personally have no love for the coyotes and I think the sooner we totally eliminate the species the better off we are . . ."

He signed his letter to me, and I'm sure he would give me permission to use his name, but I think he doesn't really mean what he wrote.

I have yet to find a rancher, no matter how virulent his hatred for the coyote, who would pull the lever if that lever absolutely eliminated all coyotes for all time to come. Sure, I have seen many men who claim that they would jump at the chance to strangle the last female coyote left in the world. I don't believe them. Their actions give them away. Too often have I seen that look of gruding admiration on their faces when they've lost another round to the coyote.

Will the coyote continue to survive the increased urbanization of America? All evidence suggests that he will not only survive, but prosper in close proximity to man. As we have already mentioned, a coyote killed a child in a Los Angeles suburb in 1981. The coyote has not yet surrendered his claim to that land which disappears under urban sprawl each year.

But what will happen when the coyote finds most of the land mass covered by man and man's works? Where then does he find a place to rear his young? Where can he find rabbits and mice and watermelons and grasshoppers and beetles and acorns and eggs and nestling birds? There is no food for the coyote when the land is covered with concrete. True, but when man takes too much land for his concrete patches, man himself will starve. It is my impression that as long as we reserve enough acreage to raise our food, we will also raise food for the clever coyote and may even find the bitch bringing up a litter of pups under the back porch of our house.

The ability to survive is the coyote's strongest and most valuable trait. Somehow, some way, he will endure. Sheep men in coyote country have long recognized this fact. When the Soviets put Sputnik in orbit with a dog passenger, and the capsule was recovered but the dog was dead, one Texas sheepman remarked—"If the Russkies had sent up a gyp coyote, not only would she have come back alive, but she'd have given birth to sixteen fat pups."

Many scientists and philosophers speak of a tendency on the part of technologically advanced civilizations to destroy themselves. Surely this civilization of ours, the most advanced the world has ever seen, has the potential for self-destruction. The possession of nuclear weapons by many nations leads one to the sorrowful conclusion that, sooner or later, some one will "try out" their weapons. If there is instant retaliation, as promised by all members of the so-called Nuclear Club, civilization will end. And possibly mankind will cease to exist.

It is my personal belief that when the last human has fallen, and the last skull lies on the irradiated earth, a coyote will come trotting out of some safe place. Don't ask me where he'll come from; but I believe that he will survive as he has always survived. The coyote will trot in his furtive, skulking manner, to the skull. He will approach it carefully with the caution borne of millennia of avoiding steel traps and snares and pitfalls. He will cautiously sniff it. His educated nose will tell him that he no longer has anything to fear from this bleached remnant of a once great civilization. Taking a few short steps to get in the exact position, he will lift his leg.

APPENDIX I

"Blown out of the prairie in twilight and dew
Half bold and half timid yet lazy all through;
Loath ever to leave, and yet fearful to stay
He limps in the clearing, an

OUTCAST IN GREY"

Bret Harte.

by Jim Keefe

One of the most maligned and controversial animals in the state of Missouri is a little carnivore laboring under the difficult name of Canis latrans Say. Most folks know him as "wolf", a more particular group call him coyote, and he has been labeled with a lot of other names, some not complimentary.

The stage for his formal introduction to white-man's life was set in 1819. At a bleak, windswept place on the Missouri river labeled Engineer Contonment, Nebraska (now known to be near the present town of Blair) a young Indiana naturalist named Thomas Say made some notes about a small "brush wolf" that had been shot nearby. He gave it the Latin name of "Barking dog"—Canis latrans. This was the wily coyote's first peek around the curtain of knowledge, his introduction to science.

There was nothing new about the coyote, really. Spanish Conquistadores had tangled with the little brute in Mexico and on the arid plains of the far west nearly three hundred years earlier. They called him "coyote" from the Indian name "coyotl." In 1804–06, Lewis and Clark made mention of him in their journals as they crawled across the immensity of the western prairies toward their ultimate goal of the Pacific Northwest. Fur

213

trappers, operating from St. Louis up along the Missouri river as far as Montana, had shot plenty of these little "prairie wolves." Early writers who accompanied fur expeditions, mention these tawny fellows that followed the buffalo herds, preying on the sick and very young. According to the accounts there must have been a lot of them. Some called them American jackals.

But science is slow and cautious. If someone hasn't published a paper, giving its official description and measurements, then a thing just doesn't exist. The coyote came into official recognition in 1823, when Say's paper was published. The first Missouri legislature, which came into existence in 1821, didn't waste a lot of time. In 1825 it enacted the original Missouri bounty law, placing a price on the head of the coyote, making him an outlaw in this state.

The coyote of Missouri is not even in the same league with the wolf that once roamed here. This was the great grey wolf, or timber wolf. In size, the wolf was easily twice as big as the average coyote, about 100 pounds and up. The Missouri coyote averages about 35 pounds, with a few going up to 50 pounds. Pioneers differentiated between them by calling one grey wolf and the other brush wolf. The coyote probably followed the grey wolf on the plains, cleaning up his buffalo kills, and living off ground squirrels and the like. Undoubtedly, he also killed his own meat, probably attacking calves and weakened animals.

Coyotes are typically a yellowish-grey color, looking a lot like a medium sized collie dog in some respects. There is a good deal of individual variation in color and general body formation, however, Coyotes have a bushy tail carried well down between the legs and seeming sometimes to be out of proportion to the body. Wolves, by contrast, generally carry their brush high when running. The coyotes head is long and narrow, with a furtive slitted expression.

He is a swift runner, much faster than the ordinary dog. Some special dog strains can overtake a coyote on clear ground, but as a fighter the coyote is more than a match for any dog near his own weight. So far as Missouri is concerned, man is the only serious enemy of the coyote. Wolves, in their range, will prey on them and eagles have been known to attack them. In turn, the coyote is the implacable foe of the bobcat.

Although his Latin name means "barking dog" the coyote is less often heard in Missouri than in his native west. He wised up quickly after man spread into this country and soon learned that survival meant keeping quiet. During mating season, which is January and February in Missouri, he can sometimes be heard barking and, at times, howling his melancholy strain, but even this is uncommon in our state. Out west the coyote's song has become a fixture, for each dawn and evening his plaintive barking wail rings out into the wide sky. Outdoorsmen there claim it would be a decided loss to the western atmosphere if the wail of the coyote were heard no more. At the same time, a good many westerners are doing all they can to make sure that this actually happens. The west is cattle and sheep country and the coyote is expendable.

At the time Thomas Say was wintering in Engineer Cantonment with the Major Stephen Long Expedition to the Rocky Mountains, the coyote occupied the area from southern Canada west to the Pacific, east to Iowa and as far south as Mexico City, including lower California. According to some authorities he had also extended his range as far south as Costa Rica.

This was the homeland of the coyote. Here he filled a niche created by nature for an animal of his propensities. In this great prairie land of the continent there flourished the large herbivores: buffalo, deer, elk, and antelope. Here also were ground squirrels, prairie dogs, and their lesser brethren, the native mice. Along with these there were the large predators such as the grey wolf, puma, and grizzly bear. In between the large predators and the smaller weasels and ferrets a niche existed for a meat-eating scavenger such as the coyote. Life must have been good, for every old account mentions the little wolf of the prairies as being very abundant! Trappers and travelers recalled the coyote as a cowardly, scavenging beast who furnished them with a good deal to laugh about and much more to cuss about.

The coyote followed this new, highly successful predator—man— robbing his meat caches and polishing off his game kills before he had a chance to prepare them for his own use. The coyote also had a peculiar love for oil and would slip into the camp area at night and chew up harness and ropes for the oil with which they had been softened.

In the wake of the explorer and trapper came the farmer with his following of stupid (by comparison with the wild animals) livestock and poultry. The coyote, ever an adaptable beast and apt at recognizing a good thing, turned some of his attention from the natural prey of the wild toward these concentrated and easily panicked animals of man. Instead of going down the sunset trail with his larger predatory neighbors, the wolf and puma, the coyote actually found things more to his liking. Food-getting became easier and the pressure of larger foes was taken off his furry neck.

Of course, some changes had to be made in his way of life. Man had a whole new bag of tricks to turn against the coyote. First he shot it when powder and ball would permit. Then he took to trapping, and even invented such devilish devices as the cyanide gun. In the latter part of the nineteenth century the great wheat area of the United States was the scene of one of the most intense strychnine poisoning operations ever carried out. Meat scraps, loaded with strychnine, were strewn across the known range of the coyote in this area and they died by hundreds of thousands. In more recent years, the 1080 poison campaign has cleared vast stretches of coyote country of this little beast, but still he pushes relentless onward into new ranges.

From his original homeland in the Rocky Mountain-Great Plains area, he has now reached the northernmost tip of Alaska and has spread eastward to the Atlantic. Even unlikely places such as Yucatan and Ontario are now reporting his presence, and every state in the Union has some record of his passing.

Undoubtedly he has spread on his own four footpads in most cases, but man himself has contributed to some of his visitations. Fox hunters on the eastern seaboard have, at times, imported "fox pups" from the west for release on hunting areas. These "foxes" turned out to be coyotes when they grew up; coyote and fox pups are difficult for the layman to distinguish. Then, too, many western visitors have brought back coyote pups for pets. They frequently find the coyote an intractable and uncertain pet when he reaches adulthood and simply turned it loose on the countryside. Naturally, a pampered pet is going to take the course of least resistance in getting food and the nearest poultry is fair game.

Foodwise, the coyote is, of course, primarily a carnivore or meat-eater. But he is indifferent to his fare and will take almost anything edible that presents itself. Leroy Korschgen, food habits specialist with the Conservation Commission, has found that the typical Missouri coyote eats rabbits mostly, with fruit, seeds, grass, along with mice and shrews running close seconds, depending on the season of the year.

Korschgen's records show that of the coyote's diet, 98.3 percent is animal in origin. By major food groups it was found that game animals are the principal source of food, because of the high proportion of rabbit found in the diet—64.6 percent average. Poultry was second in importance, but may be vastly overrated because of the eating of discarded, dead birds which properly should be classified as carrion. The same also probably applies to the livestock figure. A good deal of the livestock found in coyote diets is probably carrion and not from animals killed by the coyote. Looking over Korschgen's figures it appears that the coyote is not nearly the serious predator he is envisioned to be. The part he plays in checking rodent populations should not be overlooked in an analysis of his value, either. In the southern part of the state, cotton rats at times make up a major portion of the diet. And it is also a fact that the coyote catches a lot of blame for deeds done by roving dogs.

Coyotes apparently do not pair for life. Mating takes place in January or February and the young are born in April. Litters average about six pups, but run as high as ten or more. Coyotes appropriate dens of woodchucks or other animals, but may dig their own. Favored spots for dens are in thickets and woody field borders. Usually, they have more than one den. It is during the season when they have pups at home that they do most of their serious marauding on livestock and poultry. Pups have voracious appetites and parents are hard-pushed to fill their little maws. The fact that a lot of lambing takes place at about the same time makes it tough on some farmers.

When the young are eight to ten weeks old the den is abandoned and the entire family group roves at will. In early fall the family breaks up and each member goes its separate way. Coyotes continue their struggle against the world for about 10 to 18 years, their life span being similar to the domestic dog's.

During this 10 to 18 years the coyote has plenty of opportunity to get into a farmer or livestock raiser's hair. The fact that so few do is a cause for marvel, but that some coyotes prey on domestic animals cannot be denied, and because of this an entire species is outlawed.

As was said earlier, among the first pieces of legislation handled by a Missouri government was the passing of an authorization for bounty on coyotes. This was in 1825. Bountying coyotes has been in existence here for about 129 years. During the years 1825 to 1870 many countires had some form of bounty payment. From 1870 through 1923 the state undertook to match bounty payments of the various counties, and while this law continued on the books until 1947, with the exception of the years 1931 and 1941, no funds were appropriated by the state legislature from 1923 until last year.

In March, 1952, the legislature passed a law making it mandatory for counties to pay a bounty of $30 on adult coyotes, $5 on coyote pups. The law also provided that the state would bear two-thirds of this cost or $20 in the case of adults. Reports aren't in yet on how much this cost but here are figures for earlier years and lesser quantities.

Bounty payments in 104 Missouri counties in 1950 amounted to $54,820 on 7, 198 coyotes and 57 bobcats. In 1951, payments in 106 counties were $54,936.50 on 6,849 coyotes and 42 bobcats. This averaged out at about $8 per coyote. Just how wisely this money was spent is a matter for a great deal of argument.

One bone of contention is that bountying claims to be aimed at increasing game supplies and protecting livestock. States with the longest experience in bounty systems find no definite improvement in game or livestock conditions through such spending. No state has ever proved that bounties affected these two in any way so far as increasing or improving game or livestock conditions. Then, too, there is much fraud connected with any bounty system. Persons who pass on the validity of claims for taking coyotes or other bountied species frequently just don't know what it is all about. Few justices of the peace, county treasurers, county clerks, or for that matter, game wardens, are familiar enough with the species to unquestionably identify them, especially the young. Probably a lot of good dollars have been paid out in Missouri for fox pups, which are unbountied, under the claim that they are coyotes. The same applies to housecats passed off as bobcats.

Michigan paid $35 for adult wolf pelts at one time and a flourishing business sprang up, buying coyte skins from the Dakotas at $3 and selling them to the state of Michigan for $35. Such racketeering is frequent in states which offer bounties. States offering a high bounty rate are sure to get plenty of pelts from neighboring states whose people want to get on the gravy train.

The idea that placing a bounty on a species is going to make it attractive to the trapper as a source of cash is correct, but what most such proponents do not stop to consider is that a trapper with a business turn of mind is not going to dry up his source of income by trapping a region clean of predators. In fact, there are cases where trappers release all females so that they may breed and produce more coyotes!

Frank Sampson, furbearer biologist of the Conservation Commission, and the late Dr. Rudolf Bennitt, professor of zoology at the University of Missouri, made an exhaustive study of the bounty system in Missouri and concluded that although large numbers of predators may be taken under a bounty system it "is indiscriminate and reduces neither the material damage nor the number of complaints. In Missouri, eleven years of bounty figures offer no evidence that the population of wolves and coyotes has been reduced thereby."

All this leaves Missouri in a paradoxical situation. We've got the most progressive attitude on predator control in the country with our extension trapper program, conducted by the Commission, where farmers are taught how to trap the coyotes that harass them. At the same time the legislature of the state reverted to 1825 and passed as inviting a bounty law as it would be possible to find anywhere in the nation. Even though most states do have bounty laws on the books, some operative and some inoprative because of lack of funds, enlightened opinion has steadily swung away from the bounty system as ineffective. In the face of this, Missouri has recently passed into law an even more bountiful bounty system.

How about the coyote? Is it feeling any repercussions? Financially, there's no way of knowing until the end of the fiscal year when bounty payments are totalled. There was a splurge of scalps brought in for payment when the new bounty went into effect. Some folks were keeping them in the deep freeze, waiting for the new payments before turning them in. After that, things seemed to level off.

Biologists predict that by and large the numbers of coyotes brought in for bounty will reflect the coyote population, going up when it goes up and going down when it goes down. They expect it to have little effect on the total numbers of coyotes in Missouri. However, there is a way in which bounty money might be turned to good account in Missouri.

First of all, harken back to that money paid out in 1951 as coyote bounties. It cost an average of $8 to bring in a coyote. There was no guarantee that the coyote brought in was the same one that pulled down the farmer's sheep, but it cost eight bucks just the same. Now the state has made it mandatory to pay $30 for each coyote—almost four times as much. Here's an idea on how that money might be spent to really get the coyotes that are causing the trouble.

Funds could be set aside in each county on the same basis of apportionment: 2 to 1. The money would amount to around $205,470 on the number of coyotes bountied in 1951 and figuring $30 per animal. This would mean a fund of about $1,800 for each of the counties in the state, which could be used for coyote control. Instead of paying $30 for each animal brought in, whether it does any damage or not, this money could be used to hire, on full or part time basis, a local resident trained in predator control. There are thousands of trainees of the Commission's predator control program scattered over the state who could furnish recruits for this program. These men could be directed to the actual scene of a coyote depredation and trap for the individual animal causing damage. Too many bounty hunters go only into areas where the going is easy rather than selecting sites of actual coyote damage. In this way, the county could insure that the people's money is achieving as much predator control as possible. A county predator man might also be delegated as a farmer's agent to put down local fox damage, too.

In any system, the taxpayer is paying the bill. It seems logical that he is interested in getting the most for his money. Bounties, as such, have been shown time and again that they just don't get the job done. The simple steps outlined above may be a big step in getting real control from a predator control program and, at the same time, insure those who pay the bills that they are getting the most for their money.

No matter what kind of system is used, the fact that every man's hand is against him doesn't bother the coyote in the least. You can confidently expect that he is going to be around no matter how heavily the cards appear to be stacked against him. The very cussedness of the critter is a cause for admiration.

From his original range he has continually spread ever farther out until his paw print has been found in every state in the Union even in the face of some of the toughest opposition that could be brought to bear. And

219

remember this: the coyote is not doing any wrong—from a coyote's point of view. All he wants is a full tummy and he is going to take the course of least resistance to get it.

While it needs control, the coyote is nevertheless one of the units of nature and has a place in the Great Scheme. As a wilderness animal we just can't get along without him. Probably even his bitterest enemies might grudgingly say this: he's nice to hear when you're sitting around a campfire, just as long as he stays out of the stockpen.

Those to whom the coyote is a voice of the wild, even though they might lose some things to his furtive attack, may join with Bret Harte who finally shook his head and resignedly wrote:

"Well, take what you will—though it be on the sly,
Marauding or begging—I shall not ask why;
But will call it a dole just to help on his way
A four-footed friar in order of grey."

Jim Keefe
Missouri Conservationist
February, 1953

APPENDIX II

What Does a Coyote Eat?

The most extensive study of the coyte's diet ever completed was begun in 1931, when the Biological Survey (forerunner of the U.S. Fish and Wildlife Service) established a research laboratory in Denver to analyze stomach contents and list them both qualitatively and quantitatively.

Ten years later, Sperry published the results. It still stands as the most authoritative study of coyote foods ever performed. All in all, 14,289 coyote stomachs, obtained in every month of the year in seventeen states, were examined. The list of states includes Michigan, Wisconsin, Missouri, and all of the Western states except Oklahoma, Kansas, and North Dakota. Why it did not include my old home state of North Dakota is a mystery to me. Most of the stomachs were collected by the Biological Survey's own field personnel. Additional stomachs were obtained from the Michigan State Game Commission and from the National Park Service. Remember that the National Park Service, in the early days, had a philosophy of managing wildlife species—which often included killing some species for the benefit of others. The official policy of using only "biological" methods to reduce wildlife populations was adopted by the Park Service at a later date, and has often been winked at by practical park people who wanted to be logical in their management. For example, in the early days of the Theodore Roosevelt National Memorial Park in North Dakota, the local prairie dog population was getting out of hand, despite complete protection for predators such as the coyote and the bobcat (the biological controls which official NPS policy counted on) in the park. Park personnel, not wanting to see the prairie dogs ruin the range for the more important bison and antelope and mule deer, quietly obtained strychnine oats and reduced their prairie dog population to manageable numbers—thus effectively "balancing" the predator-prey relationship that the predators had failed to balance. But I digress. Suffice it to say that the National Park Service contributed a significant number of coyote stomachs to the Sperry study from 1931 through 1941.

The source of the stomachs, geographically, is shown below:

Arizona	513	(513)	New Mexico	1,088	(1,084)
California	863	(856)	Oregon	671	(667)
Colorado	1,101	(1,082)	South Dakota	97	(96)
Idaho	213	(208)	Texas	569	(566)
Michigan	88	(85)	Utah	178	(176)
Missouri	6	(5)	Washington	1,186	(1,179)
Montana	626	(623)	Wisconsin	7	(6)
Nebraska	70	(69)	Wyoming	918	(903)
Nevada	145	(145)			
			Totals	8,339	(8,263)

Stomachs full enough to be used in volumetric food percentages are those shown in parentheses.

Of the total (14,289) stomachs collected, 2,025 were empty, 4,368 contained only debris and 97 were from pups that were feeding on milk only, leaving 8,339 useful stomachs to be studied.

Stomachs were collected all through the year, giving a breakdown by seasons as follows: Spring 1,224 stomachs, 1,237 useable; Summer 1,641 stomachs, 1,626 useable; Fall 3,229 stomachs, 3,184 useable, and Winter 2,225 stomachs, 2,216 useable. It is not recorded which season brought in the biggest percentage of empty stomachs. One would assume that this would be winter, but that assumption might not hold true. Many stomachs were taken from coyotes which had been trapped. These animals usually had empty stomachs, as digestion continues while the trap is on the foot. According to the Sperry report, "The

Bringing a whole jackrabbit back to the den, a mother coyote feeds her young who wait in the den until she calls them out.

coyotes were primarily carnivorous at all times. During the first 4 months of the year they fed almost exclusively on flesh and even in August and September, when fruits and berries are most available, made animal food 96 percent of the diet."

Sperry reported that rabbits took first place in the diet throughout the year, except in mid-winter when they were outranked by carrion. Present in 43 percent of the stomachs, rabbits were outstanding in the coyotes food in every one of the 17 states represented. The report lists rodents (meadow mice, wood rats, cotton rats, ground squirrels, marmots, pocket mice, kangaroo rats, pocket gophers, and porcupines) separate from rabbits, and this category was in third place, following rabbits and carrion as ranked in order of importance in the coyote diet.

Big game animals in the coyote diet included antelope, bear, bison, elk, bighorn sheep and deer—deer constituted 3.58 percent.

Domestic animals identified in the coyote diet included sheep and goat remains for the most part, yet this portion of the food constituted 13 percent of the stomach contents, and was identified in one fifth of all the coyote stomachs.

The complete tabulation was:

Food Item	Percentage	Food Item	Percentage
Rabbits	33.0	Game birds	1.0
Carrion	12.0	Non-game birds	1.0
Rodents	17.5	Reptiles	(1)
Domestic Livestock		Amphibians	(1)
sheep–goat	13.0	Fishes	(1)
calf–pig	1.0	Invertebrates	
Deer	3.5	insects	1.0
Misc. Mammals	1.0	others	(1)
Poultry	1.0	Vegetable food	2.0

The Sperry report editorialized that "The coyotes' consumption of rabbits, rodents, carrion, insects, vegetable matter (in most cases) and miscellaneous mammals, which aggregated 80 percent of the diet, may be construed as not inimical to human interests or may even be considered beneficial; whereas their consumption of domestic livestock, poultry, deer and wild birds, totaling 20 percent of the food, is indicative of the loss and reveals the serious economic importance of the coyote."

The value judgements made in that paragraph might be open to question today. Who are we to say that the consumption of amphibians such as frogs, and the consumption of lizards, or skunks, is beneficial? It reminds me of the question I've been asked so many times in the last fifty years, "What good is a _____?" Fill in the blank with the name of any living creature, to suit your own prejudices. My usual answer is another question, "What good is a human?" It all depends upon your point of view.

Another, even earlier study of coyote food habits was that conducted by field men, government trappers, which was begun in 1915. The results were compiled by Henderson in 1930. While these stomach content determinations were made by untrained personnel (at least, they were untrained in the university sense), they were made by men who had an intimate knowledge of the food supply available to the coyote, men who were well acquainted with the life forms of the individual area in which they worked, and have a certain validity.

In this study, more than 30,000 coyote stomachs were studied. The stomachs were those collected in the years 1919–1923. Another 50,000 stomachs were studied, taken in the years 1924–1928. Adding the results of the two studies together wherever possible, we come up with the following totals:

Food Item	Times counted in 1919–23	Times counted in 1924–28	Total times
Beef	2,517	2,239	4,756
Sheep or goat	6,946	9,079	16,025
Pork	209	371	580
Poultry	1,306	2,705	4,011
Grouse (quail)	1,268	2,571	3,839
Waterfowl	94	136	230
Deer	399	1,209	1,608
Elk	20	72	92
Antelope	40	84	124
Rabbit	7,929	12,141	20,070
Ground squirrel	1,148	1,736	2,884
Prairie Dog	584	511	1.095
Chipmunk	65	100	165
Groundhog	64	286	354
Mouse or Rat	1,427	2,605	4,032
Insects, worms	669	542	1,211
Fish, frogs, reptiles	138	116	254

APPENDIX III

Chronology of Predator Control

Historical Dates:
U.S. Fish and Wildlife Service and Animal Damage Control

July 1, 1885   The Fish and Wildlife Service began on this date as the Section of Economic Ornithology in the Division of Entomology, U.S. Department of Agriculture. The initial appropriation was $5,000.

July 1, 1886   The Section of Economic Ornithology was made an independent division and renamed the Division of Economic Ornithology and Mammalogy. Appropriations was increased to $10,000 and several hundred questionnaires were mailed to farmers inquiring about bird damage to crops.

1887   The Division first began recommending, in letters to farmers, ground squirrel control methods developed in 1878 by Professor H. W. Hilgard, University of California at Davis. Within the Division, the Office of Economic Investigations was established.

July 1, 1896   In an attempt to establish a "systemmatic biological survey," the Division was renamed the Division of Biological Survey.

July 1, 1905   After twenty years of service as a Division or less status, Congress upgraded the organization to the Bureau of Biological Survey. The Office of Economic Investigations was changed to the Office of Economic Ornithology and Mammalogy.

1888–1914   Studies and demonstrations of animal damage control were conducted, primarily in the Western States. One organized effort was conducted by Professor Davis E. Lantz in 1912 to control prairie dogs in Pike and Cocketopa Forest in Colorado.

July 1, 1915   The first Federal direct appropriation ($125,000) for operational control of predators. As a result, nine districts were formed in the Western states and the following Predatory Animal Inspectors were appointed: C. R. Landon, Texas; Charles J. Bayer, Wyoming and South Dakota; E. W. Holman, Utah; L. J. Goldman, Idaho; E. F. Averill, Oregon; L. B. Crawford, Colorado; J. Stokley Ligon, Arizona and New Mexico; E. R. Sans, Nevada and California; and E. R. Bateman, Montana and North Dakota.

July 1, 1917   Predatory Animal Research Laboratory was established in Albuquerque, New Mexico, Sanley E. Piper, Director.

October 1, 1921   Predatory Animal Research Laboratory was moved to Denver, Colorado and the name changed to Control Methods Laboratory.

July 1, 1922   Predator animal control, including demonstrations and dissemination of information, had grown to include Arkansas, Washington, Oklahoma, Missouri, Iowa, Indiana, Louisiana, Wisconsin and Minnesota.

July 1, 1928	The Office of Economic Ornithology and Mammalogy was upgraded to division status and the name changed to the Division of Economic Investigations.
July 1, 1929	The Division was once again renamed this time to the Division of Predatory Animal and Rodent Control.
July 1, 1934	Another reorganization in Washington. The Division was combined with Law Enforcement to form the new Division of Game Management with a Section of Predator and Rodent Control.
July 1, 1938	The Section of P&RC was separated from the Division of Game Management and upgraded again to the Division of Predator and Rodent Control.
July 1, 1939	The Bureau of Biological Survey (Department of Agriculture) and the Bureau of Fisheries (Department of Commerce) were transferred to the Department of Interior by Reorganization Plan II.
July 1, 1940	The Fish and Wildlife Service was established by Reorganization Plan III, which merged the two Bureaus.
July 1, 1948	The Division of Predator and Rodent Control was renamed the Branch of Predator and Rodent Control.
July 1, 1956	Under the Fish and Wildlife Act and the Interior Reorganization Act, the U.S. Fish and Wildlife Service was increased in stature by the creation of two Bureaus, the Bureau of Commercial Fisheries and the Bureau of Sport Fisheries and Wildlife. Predator and rodent control work continued as a Branch under the Division of Wildlife.
July 1, 1965	The Service's Branch of Predator and Rodent Control was renamed the Division of Wildlife Services and given new responsibilities in

wildlife enhancement and pesticide surveillance and monitoring.

July 1, 1970   Under Reorganization Plans III and IV, the marine sport and commercial fishing functions of the Bureau of Commercial Fisheries were transferred to the Department of Commerce. Their remaining functions were either transferred to the EPA or to the Bureau of Sport Fisheries and Wildlife.

April 22, 1974   By a special act of Contress, the Bureau of Sport Fisheries and Wildlife was renamed the U.S. Fish and Wildlife Service.

May 12, 1974   The Division of Wildlife Services was abolished and the Office of Animal Damage Control was formed in accordance with the program budgeting process.

Sept. 26, 1976   The Office of Animal Damage Control was again upgraded to the Division of Animal Damage Control.

July 15, 1980   The Division was merged with the Office of Wildlife Assistance to create the new Division of Wildlife Management. In addition to ADC responsibilities, the new Division is responsible for wildlife assistance on Indian, military and other Federal agency lands and marine mammal management.

APPENDIX IV

Directors, U.S. Fish and Wildlife Service and its Predecessors

Section of Economic Ornithology

C. Hart Merriam	1885–1886

Division of Economic Ornithology and Mammalogy

C. Hart Merriam	1886–1896

Division of Biological Survey

C. Hart Merriam	1896–1905

Bureau of Biological Survey

C. Hart Merriam	1905–1910
Henry W. Henshaw	1910–1916
Edward W. Nelson	1916–1927
Paul G. Redington	1927–1934
J. N. "Ding" Darling	1934–1935
Ira N. Gabrielson	1935–1940

The Fish and Wildlife Service

Ira N. Gabrielson	1940–1946
Albert M. Day	1946–1953
John L. Farley	1953–1957

Bureau of Sport Fisheries and Wildlife

Daniel H. Janzen	1957–1965
John S. Gottschalk	1965–1971
Spencer H. Smith	1971–1973
Lynn A. Greenwalt	1973–1974

U.S. Fish and Wildlife Service

Lynn A. Greenwalt	1974–1981
Robert A. Jantzen	1981–present

APPENDIX V

Chiefs, Animal Damage Control

Section of Economic Ornithology
C. Hart Merriam   1885–1886

Division of Economic Ornithology and Mammology
C. Hart Merriam   1886–1887

Office of Economic Investigations
A. K. Fisher   1887–1905

Office Economic Ornithology and Mammalogy
A. K. Fisher   1905–1928

Division of Economic Investigations
Stanley P. Young   1928–1929

Division of Predatory Animal and Rodent Control
Stanley P. Young   1929–1934

Section of Predator and Rodent Control
Stanley P. Young   1934–1938

Division of Predator and Rodent Control
Stanley P. Young   1938–1939
Dorr D. Green   1939–1948

Branch of Predator and Rodent Control
Dorr D. Green   1948–1957
Noble E. Buell   1957–1962
Clifford C. Presnal   1962–1965

Division of Wildlife Services
Jack H. Berryman   1965–1974

Office of Animal Damage Control
Norman C. Johnson   1974–1976

Division of Animal Damage Control
Normal C. Johnson   1976–1977
Clarence E. Faulkner   1977–1980

Division of Wildlife Management
James F. Gillett   1980–present

Photo Credits